THE

IMPACT OF

CIVIL WAR

ON A COMMUNITY

Northenden and Etchells in Cheshire, 1642 – 1660

by

Jill Groves

First published in 1992
by Northern Writers Advisory Services, 77 Marford Crescent, Sale, Cheshire M33 4DN

© Jill Groves 1992

ISBN 0 9517782 1 8

Laser-printed by Northern Writers Advisory Services.

Printed by The Printing Centre, 30 Store Street, London WC1E 7BS.

CONTENTS

ILLUSTRATIONS

INTRODUCTION
Northenden and Etchells in 1642

Today the area covered by the two manors of Northenden and Etchells includes the garden-city of Wythenshawe and the adjacent villages of Northenden and Gatley, with the addition of Manchester International Airport and some green belt farm land along the southern edge. In the mid-seventeenth century the two manors were farm land, two villages (Northenden and Gatley), ten scattered settlements and two large peat moors (Shadow Moss, the larger of the two, and Northern Moor).

Over 160 tenants farmed the two manors. In Northenden there was a clearly defined four-field system. Etchells had an open field system but less well-defined.

Northenden was settled before the tenth century, the church of St Wilfrid being established there in c.900 AD, and it appears in the Domesday Book. Etchells was settled piecemeal out of woodlands in the eleventh century.

In 1297 Robert de Tatton had lands in Northenden. The demesne lands of Northenden were granted to another Robert de Tatton by his wife, Alice de Massey, daughter of William de Massey of Wythenshawe.[1] The family of Tatton of Wythenshawe rose in the mid-fifteenth century to become Barons of the Exchequer of Chester, Vice-chamberlains and sheriffs in the early sixteenth century. They intermarried with most of the notable gentry families of Cheshire, the Masseys, the Warrens, the Fittons of Gawsworth, the Booths of Dunham Massey and the Breretons of Ashley.

Etchells came into the hands of the Tattons in the mid-sixteenth century. Unlike Northenden it was made up of two townships, not one, Northen Etchells (part of the parish of Northenden) and Stockport Etchells (part of the parish of Stockport). It was so divided because in the fourteenth century the two halves of the manor had been separated. In the late fifteenth century Etchells was owned by four people, Sir William Stanley, his brother, the Earl of Derby, Sir William Booth and John Chauntrell. Later part of it was owned by the crown (after the execution for treason of Sir William Stanley in the late fifteenth century), who sold it in 1557 to William Tatton. Two years before William Tatton had bought part of the manor, Royle Thorn, from the Davenports of Henbury. Peele Hall, the manor house of Etchells, was sited on the north-eastern edge of Shadow Moss. Nearby was Chamber Hall, the courthouse for Etchells, until 1557, when it moved to Gatley.

In the seventeenth century all the tenants on the two manors were copyholders with three-life leases, paying small rents fossilised in the early sixteenth century, boons and services (which could be either in kind or money), and heriots on the death of each tenant (again either in kind or money, at the will of the lord of the manor). Many of the tenants were still living in one-roomed dwellings, although wealthier ones were beginning to add parlours and chambers.

Wythenshawe Hall, the home of the Tattons, still stands in spacious parkland near Northenden, a good example of a sixteenth/seventeenth century half-timber Cheshire hall. The remains of a moat were found during restoration work in 1953 and recently, in 1983, during more restoration, wall-paintings were discovered in the Little Dining Room, above the entrance doorway, late sixteenth century in style, in imitation of oak panelling with a painted frieze above.

A survey of Northenden manor dated March 3rd 1656/7, began with a factual description of the hall.

'Firste The scite and Mannor house called the Hall of withinshawe consistinge of a stately hall with a Dyneinge roome parlers Kitchen, Butterie, Larder, Dayrie house and Lodginge roomes, aswerable [?answerable] with a ffayre Gatehouse and other necessary roomes and places in very good and decent repare ffitt for present enjoyment.

'Allsoe to the said Mannor house and hall twoo ffayre large Barnes and a large Kill and douthouse consistinge of Eleven large bayes of buildinge well covered with slate and in good order and a large stable with other roomes thereto necessary allsoe in good plight and order fit for presente imployment, and well covered with slate, a large Oxehouse and Cowhouse with an ordinary stable and a large Granarie over it, and allsoe divers other Bayes of good buildinge for all maner of necessaries for housekeepers in good repaire Together with Banqueting house of Bricke and slated and walles there unto belonging in decent order.

'Allsoe twoo Large Orchardes, the one lately planted with Choice ffruite trees severall gardens with many outlandish ffruite trees and other trees and plants vines flowers and herbes, and other garden plants with Inner Courtes Fouldes and yardes containeinge aboute ffour Acres of Land by Cheshire'.[2]

Notes
1. G. Ormerod, *History of Cheshire*, Helsby edition, vol.1, published by E.J. Morten, Didsbury, facsimile of 1882 edition (1980) (originally published in 1882 as Vol.III), p.605.
2. John Rylands Library (J Ry L) Tatton Family Papers, no.222; W.H. Shercliffe, editor, *Wythenshawe: Volume 1 to 1926*, E.J. Morten, Didsbury, 1974, pp.78-79

The Tatton Family of Wythenshawe Hall in 1642

Background to the Civil War in Cheshire

Long before the Civil War the Cheshire gentry were divided into two parties because of a dispute over who had precedence at the Quarter Sessions, the Baronets (a title created by James I in the early 1600s) or the Barons (those who had bought Scottish or Irish titles from Charles I). When civil war came to Cheshire, with a few exceptions, the Royalists were drawn from the supporters of the Barons and the Parliamentarians from the supporters of the Baronets. The most notable exception was Sir William Brereton, the darling MP of the Barons in the Short Parliament.

Despite the events of Christmas 1641, the King's ignominious flight from London and the preparations for war, the Cheshire gentry believed that the Long Parliament and the King should come together. In the late summer of 1642 Sir George Booth of Dunham, an indomitable old man of seventy-six, established with other members of the gentry a demilitarised, non-alignment campaign. In December the same year, with the First Civil War begun but not yet in full, ferocious flood, Sir George Booth, Lord Kilmorrey and others drew up a declaration of neutrality called the Treaty of Bunbury. But the treaty failed. Within a month Royalist forces led by Sir Thomas Aston, and Parliamentarian forces under the command of Sir William Brereton entered the county. The first battle in Cheshire, the first battle of Nantwich, was fought in January 1643.

Before the arrival of Sir Thomas Aston and Sir William Brereton happenings in Manchester in the summer and autumn of 1642 had alarmed Royalists in East Cheshire, and a number of them took up arms when Lord Strange laid siege to the town in late September.

After the battle of Nantwich Cheshire was not a place for neutrals, as Edmund Joydrell of Yeardsley and William Davenport of Bramhall discovered. They were threatened by Parliamentarian and Royalist neighbours, their estates were plundered by the armies of both sides, and lastly they were declared delinquents by the Macclesfield Sequestration Committee and heavily fined.

Robert Tatton and his Family

By October 1642 Robert Tatton was a committed Royalist. He had been a captain in the Macclesfield Trained Band in the 1630s, so probably on his own initiative, although he may have been commissioned by Sir Thomas Legh of Adlington, High Sheriff of Cheshire, who lived only half a day's ride from Wythenshawe, he raised men for Lord Strange's siege of Manchester. After the failure of the siege in early October he and Thomas Legh fortified their homes in the name of the King. This was done at a time when many Cheshire people still hoped the conflict could be resolved peacefully.

From the evidence of the Wythenshawe garrison list, Robert Tatton had considerable local influence, rivalling that of Sir George Booth.[1] Over half the listed members of the garrison came from outside his manors.

A study of Robert Tatton's family and marriage connections reveals a certain amount of polarisation amongst his relatives. In general, Robert's side of the family were Royalists, whereas those on his wife's side were Parliamentarians – at least at the beginning of the war.

Anne Tatton's eldest brother, Richard, aged fifty-two in 1642, was a JP and a regular attender at the Quarter Sessions prior to 1640s. During the period 1640-2 he was one of the leading 'Baronets'.[2] At the end of August he and other moderates wrote to Lord Strange complaining that:-

'the country is putt in feare not onely by sevrall meetings of the Commissioners of Array for this County amongst themselves but alsoe w[i]th Com[missione]rs of other Countys adiaecent, And that some of them have given out threatenings and desparate language, that they would plunder, batter downe, burne the houses and disarme the persons of all such as complie not w[i]th them in their way, thoughe otherwise have taken the protestacon to be aideing to King and Parliament... al w[hi]ch speeches and undertakings wee conceive to bee expressly contrary to his Matys frequently declaracons for the maintenance of the right and property of the subject.'[3]

Lord Strange's reply was addressed to Richard Brereton and his friend, Henry Mainwaring of Kermincham, and whilst not denying its charges, was soothing in its tone.

'I assure you there is noe such direconn or consent or myne, But contrariwise I shall send unto them to beware thereof, with this declaration, that if they doe contrarie to my owne request unto them, I will take part with others against them.'[4]

Thomas, Richard's junior by four years, was more radical, although he did not really come to the fore in Cheshire politics until after his brother's death in 1649 when he became a Commissioner of the Peace.[5]

Peter, the youngest of the three surviving brothers, was born in 1601. He was a lawyer and his politics may have been similar to those of his brother Thomas. He was a friend of John Bradshawe of Marple, Lord President of the High Court in 1648/49 with some influence in the House of Commons. Bradshawe mentioned Peter Brereton in his will in 1659, calling him 'my good freind' and cousin.[6] It could be that Peter's connection with John Bradshawe meant that he was more radical than Thomas. Perhaps he was also one of Sir William Brereton's nominees.

Anne's eldest sister, Frances, born 1592, married Alexander Barlowe of Barlowe, when she was forty-one. He was sixteen years her junior and came of a Lancashire Roman Catholic family. His uncle, Edmund, trained as a Benedictine priest in France at Valladoid and Douai. Taking the Catholic name Ambrose, he worked as a missionary in Lancashire amongst the many Catholic families for twenty years. Father Ambrose was imprisoned several times before being executed at Lancaster on September 10th, 1641. Later he

FAMILY TREE OF THE TATTONS OF WYTHENSHAWE HALL

(taken from Earwaker's family tree of the Tattons reprinted in "Wythenshawe:
Volume 1 to 1926" p.47-51. Only surviving offspring are listed)

```
            ROBERT TATTON m (1) Ellen, 3rd dau. of John Warren of
of Wythenshawe. Died at      Poynton, Cheshire, Esq. c.1583
Southwark, 10 Jan        (2) Susan, dau. of ?
1623-4                        |
                              |
    _____
    |                              |                    |
WILLIAM TATTON m Katherine, dau of  Elizabeth          Mary
Bapt Sept 15     Sir Geo. Leycester Bapt April 19,     Living 1603
1585. Marr       of Toft. Remarried 1587 Marr at       Marr...Ognell
1602-3           Dr. Nicholls Jan   Didsbury, May 25
Drowned in the   27 1628-29. Bur    1617, John Latham
Mersey Jan 8     Jan 13 1665-6      of Hawthorne Hall.
1616-17          |                  Remarried 1622 Geo.
                 |                  Mainwaring of Marthall,
                 |                  2nd son of Sir Randle M.
                 |                  of Peover
    _____
    |                              |                    |
ROBERT TATTON m Anne Brereton, 3rd  Margaret            Eleanor
Bapt May 19,     dau of William     Bapt April 15       Bapt May 6
1606             Brereton of Ashley 1610. Marr to       1612. Marr
                 Esq. Marr at       Richard Twyford     Edward
                 Bowdon Jan 9       of Didsbury         Legh of
                 | 1628-9                               Baguley, Esq.
                 |
    _____
    |         |           |           |         |          |
  Mary      Anne        WILLIAM     Robert    Richard     Thomas
Born Dec 24 Born Aug 4  Born July   Born April Twin with  Thomas
1629        1632        9 1636      25 1639    Bapt. May 18 1642
```

was canonised as St. Ambrose.

Why then did Alexander Barlowe become a Protestant? He may have been under a great deal of pressure from officials and friends to change, but on the other hand his own family would have wanted him to remain true to the old religion. Whenever he made this momentous decision it was before 1633, the year in which he married Frances Brereton. She came from a moderate Puritan family. Her brothers would not have been too pleased if she married a Catholic. Barlowe did later become an important, though moderate, member of the Parliamentary Commissioners in Manchester, 1649-1656.

Barlowe knew Humphrey Chetham, a Lancashire clothier and sheriff of Lancashire in 1649. In 1651 he became, along with Richard Holland of Denton (Sir William Brereton's cousin), and other worthies of Manchester, one of the governors, or feoffees, of Humphrey Chetham's Hospital, a school for twelve poor boys set up in the fifteenth century manor house of Manchester by Chetham's will in 1653 (it became the famous Chetham's School of Music in the 1950s).[7]

Katherine, Anne's youngest sister, married Ralph Assheton of Kirkby in Yorkshire. He became Sir Ralph Assheton of Whalley and his son was MP for Clitheroe. His nephew, also Ralph Assheton of Middleton, was MP for Lancashire and Commander-in-Chief of the Lancashire Parliamentarian forces.

So, of her own family, Anne was the only one to espouse the Royalist cause.

Robert Tatton's mother, Katherine, had a younger sister, Mary, who married James Massey of Sale, her father's ward, in 1611. James was charged as a delinquent by the Macclesfield Sequestration Committee but this is the only evidence that he might have had Royalist sympathies (he was a Catholic so he may have been charged as a matter of course). He may helped his nephew gather food and arms to help garrison Wythenshawe, but there is no extant record of this. However, his son Richard, Robert's cousin, had a disagreement with Sir William Brereton in 1635 which might be another reason why he and his father were harshly treated after the First Civil War.[8]

Katherine's other sister, Alice, married John Bradshawe of Bradshawe, a distant Lancashire cousin of the regicide judge. Her son, also John Bradshawe, became a Parliamentarian Lieutenant-Colonel in the Lancashire forces under Ralph Assheton. In 1643 he was a deputy lieutenant for the county.

Ralph Leycester of Toft, the only surviving brother, died in 1640, leaving his son, George, as head of the family. Nothing is known of the politics of Katherine's nephew, except by negative deduction. No Leycester of Toft appears in the undated schedule of Royalist delinquents printed in Ormerod, *History of Cheshire*, Volume 1, p.LXIII. But his cousin, Peter Leycester of Tabley, a famous Cheshire historian and antiquarian in the Restoration period, was a Royalist. Perhaps George, like many others, bowed to pressure from Sir George Booth and sided with the Parliamentarians. Certainly another cousin, Richard Leycester of Toft, was a Parliamentarian.[9]

Twelve years after the death of her first husband and eighteen days after the wedding of her son Robert, Katherine Tatton married Dr William Nicholls, rector of Cheadle. Nicholls, then aged thirty-six (six years younger than his wife) with a doctorate from Cambridge, had been presented to the living at Cheadle in 1624 by Charles, Prince of Wales (Richard Bulkeley of Cheadle, who held the advowson, was then a minor). Nicholls did not live at Cheadle until after the death of his curate, Edward Berron, and probably not even then. Berron and his family occupied the parsonage.[10] From 1637-1651 Berron's successor was the Puritan curate, Francis Shelmerdine of Chamber Hall, Etchells (later to

THE FAMILY OF THE BRERETONS OF ASHLEY

WILLIAM BRERETON m Jane, dau of Peter Warburton
of Arley

RICHARD	Thomas	William	Peter	
Bapt Dec	Bapt 26 March	Bapt 23rd Dec	Bapt 26 Aug	
1590	1594. Marr	1596 D.1632	1601 D.1659	
Sheriff	Theodosia,			
of Ches.	dau of Sir			
1632 14	Thomas Tirrell			
Sept 1649				
}				
William,				
son of Ellen				
Higginson,				
Richard's servant				

Frances	Anne	Katherine
Bapt 26 Aug 1592	Bapt 6 June	Bapt 16 March
Marr Alexander Barlowe	1597 Marr Robert	1598 Marr
of Barlowe in 1633	Tatton in 1629	Raufe Ashton
		of Kirkby, younger
		son of Sir
		Richard Ashton
		of Middleton

be chaplain to Robert Duckenfield's and Henry Bradshawe's Parliamentarian regiments). But it seems likely from the evidence of one document that Shelmerdine did not occupy the parsonage either. Dr Nicholls was better housed at the Peele Hall, his wife's dower house. A document amongst the Tatton Family Papers shows Dr Nicholls was closely involved in the farming of his wife's estate and tenancies, something it would have been hard to do on a daily basis from Cheadle.

William Nicholls was, like his step-son, a staunch Royalist. Early in 1641 he was sitting in Petty Sessions as a JP in January 1641 at Chester; next at Nantwich in July with Sir Edward Fitton and Thomas Stanley, the former a member of the 'Barons'' party, the latter belonging to the 'Baronets' and later a Parliamentarian. Nicholls may have been part of what J.S. Morrill calls the 'Barons'' plan to take over the Petty and Quarter Sessions as the conflict between the King and Parliament grew in 1641.[11]

Robert Tatton's eldest sister, Margaret, married Richard Twyford of Didsbury. He was born in 1610, the third son of John and Alice Twyford. According to the Manchester Committee for Sequestrations his property was valued at £440, the estate of a minor gentleman.[12] There is no evidence about his political affiliations before the Civil War but he and his elder brother, Robert, joined Robert Tatton's garrison at Wythenshawe in November 1643.[13]

Robert Twyford was a steward of the Manchester Court Leet sometime before 1643. He was, like most seventeenth century stewards of court leets, a lawyer and had a Manchester practice. Through his wife, Margaret, daughter of the clothier, Alexander Radcliffe of Manchester, Twyford had important connections with the wealthier citizens of Manchester, including the clothier, Humphrey Chetham.[14]

As members of the parochial gentry, involved with local government, the Twyfords might have been expected join the Parliamentarians. Most of the Parliamentarians around Manchester were drawn from such petty gentry, lawyers and merchants.

Richard Twyford's name appears on the Protestation Returns sent from parish to parish by Richard Heyricke, the Presbyterian Warden of the collegiate church of Manchester.[15] But too much should not be read into this. Nine others whose names appear on the list of the Wythenshawe garrison also signed the Protestation.

Richard was involved in a small scandal in 1636 when, after four years of marriage to Margaret, he fathered a child on a tenant farmer's daughter, Elizabeth Coppocke.[16] A woman bearing an illegimate child in the seventeenth century would be driven out of her parish, unless she was betrothed or handfasted, which was then considered more important than the actual marriage ceremony. Between Northenden and Didsbury parishioners there were close family ties. So Elizabeth Coppocke had her baby daughter baptised in Northenden, after giving birth in the house of her cousins.[17]

Eleanor, the younger of Tatton's sisters, married Robert's near neighbour Edward, the second son of Henry Legh of Baguley. His father died in 1634 and his grandfather Richard in 1641. In August 1642 Edward's elder brother, Richard died and he inherited the Baguley estates. Later Richard's widow, Brigit, a member of the influential Parliamentarian family the Harringtons, claimed a large portion of the Baguley estates. Although an old established family (the Leghs of Baguley were the senior branch), they seemed not to rank as high amongst the county elite as their cousins, Sir Thomas Legh of Adlington and Peter Legh of Lyme. The Leghs of Baguley seemed to have declined to a status below that of Robert Tatton, yet still part of the county elite, above the parochical gentry.

So by September 1642 only Robert Tatton, Dr Nicholls and the Brereton brothers definitely supported one or the other side before hostilities began in October 1642. It would be unfair to say that the rest drifted either towards the Royalists or the Parliamentarians according to who was in the ascendency in their area. Many Royalists in Cheshire and elsewhere were complacent about their ultimate victory. In Cheshire and Lancashire their strength was greater than that of the Parliamentarians in October 1642, so they thought they would naturally win without much effort. After all, God was on their side. But by January 1643 the Parliamentarians were equal in numbers to the Royalists. In Lancashire

3

the Earl of Derby had not been able to subdue radical South Lancashire and Manchester as he hoped.

Robert Tatton's economic affairs prior to 1642

Because of his father's early death from drowning when he was only ten, Robert was made a crown ward, which meant that until he was twenty-one the crown, or whoever was appointed as his guardian, could enjoy the rents and profits from Northenden and Etchells manors, giving an allowance to Robert and his sisters. His mother had her dowry portion of Peel Hall and the lands around it in the south of Etchells manor. This, combined with the large fine paid when the ward came of age, as well as the heriot, and a further fine of 200 marks or £66 13s 4d when Robert Tatton married in January 1628/29, could have put his estates into debt for a good few years. Wythenshawe Hall was already mortgaged and Katherine Tatton, Robert's widowed mother, had borrowed £344 19s 6d. from Edmund Joydrell of Yeardsley. He was given 18 acres of Peele demesne land and the Chamber Hall tenement rent free for life in part payment.[18]

The fact that Robert Tatton was a crown ward at all reveals an odd set of family circumstances. Robert's grandfather was still alive in 1617 when William Tatton was drowned in the River Mersey, and so ordinarily the estates would not have come to his grandson until his death in 1623. Robert the grandfather did not fully inherit Wythenshawe after the death of his father William in 1611. Perhaps it was in an effort to lessen the fine on his own death. An inquisition on his father, William the elder, reveals that there were considerable entailments to uncles, brothers and cousins. Even in 1670 Tatton cousins were living in a tenement in Northenden, almost rent free, as a result of the entailments. But it might also have been due to a strained relationship with his father. Robert the grandfather was ignored in the lifetime of his own father, as evidenced in some documents. But he seems to have gained the control over the estates that his father's settlement denied him. Several court leets and court barons were conducted in his name.

Then in 1616 he went to live in London with his second wife, Susan. In the same year, less than a month before William the younger drowned in the Mersey, the hall and demesne lands were mortgaged to Thomas Goodyear, citizen and draper of London, to be redeemed on payment of £556 on May 20th, 1618. Thomas Goodyear discharged Robert Tatton of £100 of the debt on May 1636.[19]

Mortgages and heriot fines on the hall and manors meant that Robert Tatton had to borrow more money. In 1640 the Court of Wards and Liveries was still serving warrants and decrees against him for non-payment of debts incurred during his minority.[20]

With his brother-in-law, Richard Brereton, standing surety, Tatton borrowed £600 from his friend, Thomas Gerrard of the Riddings, Timperley, in 1635. By 1641 Richard had repaid £300 of that money, for which Robert Tatton granted him 25 acres of demesne land, the Northen Parks, for thirty-one years. The rest of the money was still unpaid in 1648, which at 8% interest meant a repayment of £420. Tatton also borrowed £70 from Richard's younger brother, Thomas, in May 1636.[21]

Robert Tatton had a growing family in the 1630s and a large household to maintain. The yearly rents from his tenants, including heriots and monies in lieu of boons and services, amounted to £308 per year. Entry fines on new leases might have increased the income to over £400. The demesne farm provided all food and most of the drink for the household, and the profits from cheesemaking, cattle and corn sold at market probably produced another £100 a year. Set against this were not only the expenses of a large household and twenty or thirty outdoor servants but the dramatic increase in food prices up to the 1640s – 70% up from the 1580s. This was partly due to the great increase in the population from 1580 to 1620s and the decline in some of England's industries, especially the cloth industry, which was important to the economy of Northenden and Etchells.

Robert Tatton improved his land by methods used since the late Middle Ages. Marl, a limy clay, was taken from pits on Northern Moor and spread over fields as a fertiliser during their fallow year, along with manure. The 1641 map shows at least ten fields under marl. At the same time he was also making improvements to the drainage of land in the flood plain of the River Mersey, adding three or four new fields for possible arable cultivation. The Court Leet/Court Baron of Northenden frequently called on the tenants to repair their water banks and gripyards to stop the Mersey from flooding the land too much (some flooding was desireable as in the case of water meadows).

It is possible that if Robert Tatton had been able to carry on with his improvements on the Northenden and Etchells manors by the 1650s he and his tenants would have been able to produce enough surplus cheese, arable products and coal to supply the growing trade centres of Manchester and Stockport, giving a handsome profit. But the financial effect of the Civil War was to put the Tatton family and their estates into a decline from which they did not recover until the early eighteenth century when they once again bought up land, enclosed and improved their estates. As a landowner and farmer, the Civil Wars were an economic disaster of the first magnitude to Robert Tatton.

Notes

1. Wythenshawe garrison list printed in J.P. Earwaker, *East Cheshire: Past and Present*, Vol 1. (afterwards Earwaker).
2. John Morrill, *Cheshire 1630-1660: County Government during the English Revolution*, Oxford University Press, p.61.
3. BL Harleian ms, quoted in *Cheshire 1630-1660*.
4. Ibid.
5. CCRO Cowper mss, vol.2, f.1.
6. John Bradshawe's will in *East Cheshire; Life of Humphrey Chetham*, Chetham Society, New Series, Vol 49, p.174, letter no. 12.
7. Ibid, Part II, Vol 50, p.332.
8. Leycester of Toft Family pedigree from Ormerod, Vol 1; N.V. Swain, *A History of Sale*, p.42.
9. *Cheshire 1630-1660*.
10. Earwaker, Vol 1, p.220.
11. *Cheshire Quarter Sessions*, The Record Society of Lancashire and Cheshire (LCRS), Vol 94; *Cheshire 1630-1660*.
12. LCRS, Vol 95.

13. Printed in Earwaker, vol.1.

14. J.P. Earwaker, editor, *Manchester Court Leet Records*, vol.IV (Manchester).

15. Protestations Returns, February, 1642 – Warden Heyricke's Protestation. Those who signed the Didsbury petition are listed in Frances Woodall, *A New History of Didsbury*, pp.28-30.

16. *St James's Didsbury, Parish Register*, published by Parish Register Society of Lancashire and Cheshire, Vol 1, Part 1, 1900.

17. Ibid and the unpublished parish register of St Wilfrids' Northenden, vol.1.

18. J Ry L Tatton Family Papers, no. 213.

19. 'Cheshire Inquisition Post-Mortems, 1603-1660', *LCRS*, vol.91; J Ry L Tatton Family Papers, no. 379.

20. J Ry L Tatton Family Papers, nos.258, 378 and 380.

21. J Ry L Tatton Family Papers, no.1284 – the granting of Northen Parks to Richard Brereton; Earwaker, Vol 1, reprinted delinquency assessment for the fine. There is also a copy amongst Humphrey Chetham's papers, Chetham's Library, Manchester; J Ry L Tatton Family Papers, nos.398-400.

The Beginnings of Unrest

Events in Cheshire and South Lancashire, June to September 1642

On June 14th an attempt was made by the sheriff of Lancashire, Sir John Girlington, and the Lord Lieutenant of Lancashire, Lord Strange, to seize the gunpowder and match stored in Manchester. The attempt failed partly because Ralph Assheton of Middleton, MP of Lancashire, and a deputy lieutenant, Sir Thomas Stanley, had removed the ammunition from its customary place in the collegiate buildings.

After this incident Manchester was the scene of many scuffles and fights between Parliamentarians, who claimed the town as their own, and local Royalists. In mid-July Lord Strange and Sir Alexander Radcliffe of Ordsall, whilst holding a meeting of Royalists at the 'Eagle and Child' in Manchester, were forced to flee from a great Parliamentarian crowd.

Lord Strange took this incident as a personal insult and the Manchester Parliamentarians took precautions, even engaging the services of an experienced military engineer, Colonel John Rosworm.[1]

Attempts by the Commissioners of Array in Cheshire to muster the Trained Bands at Northwich in mid-August were forestalled by the Parliamentarian Sir William Brereton of Handforth who summoned them to Ranmore. The arrival of King Charles in Chester on September 22nd put new heart into all Cheshire Royalists and gave Lord Strange the impetus he needed to attack Manchester.

It is possible that Robert Tatton recruited a company of sixty or seventy soldiers from amongst tenants and freeholders in the surrounding areas to help Lord Strange. Ormerod mentions that he helped to keep open the communications between Warrington, Lord Strange's starting point, and Manchester. A year later Robert had three Manchester Royalists in his garrison at Wythenshawe. They probably joined him during the siege of Manchester.[2]

The siege began the day the King entered Chester, September 22nd, and ended a week later on October 1st. Royalist cannon attacked along Deansgate and across Salford Bridge. There was a skirmish at Market Stead Lane and Long Millgate, the eastern edge of the town, but the Royalists were repulsed at every turn by the townsfolk. The Royalists suffered heavy losses, and finally at the end of the week Lord Strange withdrew.

Many reasons have been put forward for Lord Strange's failure. The weather was very wet and demoralising, the losses great and, apart from Robert Tatton and his company, there was little support from Cheshire Royalists. Sir Thomas Legh of Adlington raised a company but he could not persuade his men to cross into Lancashire. Cheshire Parliamentarians, like the Booths of Dunham, sent men and supplies to the Manchester garrison.

After he marched away from Manchester, Lord Strange (now Earl of Derby following the death of his father), sent troops commanded by Lord Molyneux of Sefton and Charles Gerard south to join the King. But he himself remained in Lancashire, recruiting for the King. Broxap and others have argued that if Manchester had fallen to Lord Derby then the Royalist cause would have been supreme in Lancashire and Cheshire. It was the fall of Cheshire so early on to the Parliamentarians, at a time when the Royalists were victorious elsewhere, that proved to be the turning point.[3]

Robert Tatton returned home to begin fortifying Wythenshawe Hall.[4] Thomas Leigh turned back from Stockport to do the same at Adlington. The failure of the siege of Manchester meant that they were two small, isolated Royalist enclaves in strongly Parliamentarian East Cheshire.

The Fortifying of Wythenshawe Hall, November 1642 – November 1643

According to a statement made by one of his tenants in 1646, Robert Tatton began fortifying Wythenshawe from November 1642 onwards 'to preserve the house and his goods from spoyle and plunder of all partyes'.[5]

There were very strong reasons why Robert Tatton and Thomas Legh, as staunch Royalists, needed to fortify their houses: the failure of Lord Strange's desultory attempt to capture Manchester; Sir George Booth's decision to support the Parliamentarian cause; and the influence of Sir William Brereton of Handforth, the Puritan MP, resulted in Macclesfield Hundred and the eastern half of Bucklow Hundred becoming strongly Parliamentarian. Then the Royalist policy in Cheshire resulted in the concentration of resources upon Chester. After the defeat of Sir Thomas Aston at Middlewich in March 1643 this meant that most of the county was left in Parliamentarian hands. Naturally such a situation contributed to the Royalists' downfall in Cheshire in 1644.

When the King departed Chester in late September 1642, accompanied by two regiments of foot, Rivers and Fitton, and three troops of horse, Aston's amongst them, Robert Tatton and Thomas Legh must have felt very isolated in Parliamentarian East Cheshire, but neither heeded the order for Royalist gentry to move into Chester for their own protection.[6] Like the Commissioners of Array, they opposed the city leaders. The Commissioners thought a more realistic policy with a wider recruiting area and financing base would be better. Paradoxically, four years later, as acting High Sheriff of Cheshire, Robert Tatton was to work beside one of the formulators of that Royalist policy, the mayor Charles Walley, whilst negotiating with Sir William Brereton for the surrender of Chester in January 1646.

From November 1642 onwards sympathetic neighbours began bringing weapons and food to Wythenshawe Hall. The moat was cleared of all accummulated dead leaves, grass and weeds. Robert also had access to the arms and gunpowder of a Trained Band company.

The Wythenshawe Garrison

The list of the Wythenshawe Garrison.

'The persons hereunder named went into, were or were sent to Garrison att Wythenshawe against the Parliament, viz, Thomas Mallory, clerke, Robert Twyford and Richard his brother; Henry Pendleton of Manchester; Edward Carter, clerke, and William Carter, the organist at Manchester; Edward Legh of Baguley, Esq; Mr. Richard Vawdrey; Mr. John Bretland and his man. And theise inhabitants of Northerden; James Renshall, Henry and Robert his sonnes; Humphrey Savage, Thomas Hampson, Henry Coppocke, James Deane, Edmund Prestwych and his two sons Edmund and John, Roger Rowson of Kenerden, Raphe and James Brownhill of the Moorside, John Poween of the Moorside. Out of Baguley, Wm. Hamnet, Robert Chapman and Nicholas his brother, Thomas Hill. Out of Gatley, Raphe Savage, Robert Torkinton, and John Blomiley. Out of Etchells, William Bailey and his sonne. Out of Didsbury, Henry Tipping, Alexander Coppocke, William Piggott. One William Clarke and John Blomiley were in the Garrison.

'And also that Robert Deane of Altrincham, Hugh Newton, Richard Grantham of Hale, Robert his sonne, George Delahey of Timperley, Andrew Winterbotham, alias Pole, and his brother Raph, Lawrence Hardy, Thomas Barlowe, John Cockson of Sharson greene in Northenden, William Hopwood, Richard Smith, Henry Bannister, Laurence Walker of Didsbury, and Thomas Lynney of the same, were in the said Garrison.'[7]

This list was compiled sometime between March 1644 and 1647 – up to three years after the end of the siege – from depositions taken from Tatton servants and tenants, probably under duress in Stockport Prison, by the Macclesfield Sequestration Committee. It must have been hard for them to remember who was there and who was not so long after the event and when so much else had taken place in the intervening time.

So there are people are on this list who were probably not at Wythenshawe at the time of the siege. John Bretland of Thorncliff strenuously claimed that he was there fifteen months before the siege only as agent to Sir George Booth, to persuade Robert Tatton not to raise troops for the Royalist cause. Between 1643 and 1649 there was a running feud between the Deputy Lieutenants of Cheshire, of whom Sir George Booth was the most prominent, against Sir William Brereton. John Bretland was the Deputy Lieutenants' candidate for the position, which ultimately went to Brereton's nominee, John Bradshawe of Marple, of Lord President of the Council of State. So the radicals waged a vindictive campaign against Bretland, which they could not have done against his patron, using a slight chink in his armour to pull him down. He was charged with delinquency. Bretland took seven long hard years to clear his name, then died from exhaustion the following year.[8]

There are also names missing from the list. One deponent declared that 'there came divers ffootemen to the s[aid]d Garrison w[hi]ch hee this dep[onen]t did not see but heard of, and nowe hath forgotten'. William Smith of Shadow Moss, a substantial tenant, compounded for his delinquency on the grounds that he was part of the garrison, yet his name does not appear on the list.[9] For the purposes of this study it will be assumed that all the men mentioned in the list, with the exception of John Bretland and his man, were members of the garrison.

Let's begin by breaking the garrison down into social groups. The total was fifty-two, including Robert Tatton. By far the largest social group were the twenty-five servants and tenants – the men of Northenden, Baguley,

Gatley, Etchells and Didsbury, those who had little choice but to go with their masters, Tatton, Legh and the Twyford brothers. Tatton provided seventeen from his tenants in Northenden and Gatley, Edward Legh four from Baguley, and the Twyford brothers possibly five from Didsbury.

The next largest group were the sixteen freeholders, who joined of their own free will. These men were geographically wide-ranging, from Didsbury to Altrincham to Timperley to Hale. Two of them, the Granthams, father and son, deserve closer investigation. Richard Grantham and his twelve year old son, Robert, came from Davenport Green Hall (built by his father, John Grantham in 1611), near Halebarns. The Granthams were a rising yeoman family. After the Civil Wars they called themselves gentlemen. They were also at this time a divided family. Whilst Richard supported Robert Tatton and his brother Ralph supplied some of the garrison's food stuffs, his uncle or cousin, Richard Grantham of Cheadle, was a captain in the regiment of Colonel George Booth (the grandson of old Sir George Booth). With Captain Alcocke, also of Cheadle, he commanded a country company of 100 foot soldiers. Later he served under Colonel Henry Bradshawe.[10]

Another man who had his family loyalties divided was John Cockson of Sharston Green, a close kinsman of Henry Cockson, the Parliamentarian Solicitor for Sequestrations in Cheshire. Both Lawrence Walker and Thomas Lynney of Didsbury signed Heyricke's Protestation in February 1642.[11] They were not the only members of Tatton's garrison to do so. Richard Twyford, Tatton's brother-in-law, signed, as did Alexander Coppocke, William Piggott and John Blomeley. But which John Blomeley is meant is a puzzle. The Blomeleys were a very numerous family living in Didsbury and Northenden. Three John Blomeleys signed the Protestation. Either Twyford and the rest were forced to sign or they later changed their minds. The latter is the more probable.

The third largest group was the clerics and schoolmasters, at the surprisingly large number of five, including a son (eight year old Thomas Bayley). Two, Edward Carter and his brother William, were refugees from Manchester, from the Collegiate Church. Perhaps they fought with Lord Strange's troops and were taken under Robert Tatton's protection soon after the failure of the siege.

The most eminent of the clerics was Mr. Thomas Mallory, the rector of Northenden, a newcomer to the district. He was the fourth son of Dr Mallory, Dean of Chester 1606-1644, rector of Davenham (1601-1644) and Mobberley (1621-1644), and Elizabeth Vaughan, daughter of Bishop Vaughan of Chester. Thomas was the fourth son but the second son of that name to be born to Dr Mallory at Davenham so his birth date is often assumed to have been that of his elder brother, Thomas, who was born in 1605 but who died as an infant. The third son, William, was not born until 1606, so the surviving Thomas Mallory junior might not have been born until 1607 or more probably 1609, after the birth of his sister Elizabeth.[12]

Thomas Mallory junior was a graduate of New College, Oxford, matriculating when he was twenty. In any other century, with his education and connections in the Church, Thomas Mallory would have risen quickly taking over his father's position as Dean and perhaps becoming a bishop. But during the 1620s and 1630s a large number of highly educated young clergymen were turned out by the universities of Oxford and Cambridge, far more than there were vacant livings. The problem could have been solved by a little re-organisation of the parish boundaries. These were small units in the south, but in the north, Cheshire and Lancashire especially, they were ridiculous large. Many contemporaries commented that some villages in the north did not even know Christianity. Archbishop Laud planned to make changes in the parish boundaries along with all his other changes in Church structure, but because of his unpopular Arminianist policies, he was swept from power and into the Tower at the beginning of the Long Parliament in November 1640.[13]

Thomas Mallory senior produced a very large family of eight sons and four daughters. Two sons, Thomas and George, became churchmen and two daughters married clergymen. Dean Mallory was a wealthy man. He bought the advowson of Mobberley Church in 1619, and the manor-house and part of the demesne of Mobberley in 1625. In November 1642 Dean Mallory was evicted from his manor-house and his livings by the Parliamentarians and went to live in the Deanery at Chester, where he died on April 3rd, 1644, aged seventy-eight.

Three of the Mallory sons, Richard the eldest, William the third son, and Thomas espoused the Royalist cause. In fact, William Mallory was knighted at Edgehill, October 1642.

Besides family connections, Thomas Mallory had the patronage of William Forster, rector of Northenden 1627-1635, and Barrow, 1602-1635, Bishop of Sodor and Man (himself under the patronage of the Earl of Derby) 1633-34. In 1634 Forster bequeathed the living of Northenden to Thomas Mallory junior, the advowson of which was given to Richard Mallory, and William Forster, nephew of the Bishop. On Bishop Forster's death Thomas Mallory was presented to the living of Northenden (this was done twice in February and August 1635 because the title of those holding the advowson was not immediately accepted).[14]

Between his matriculation and his appointment to the living of Northenden, Thomas Mallory junior was a curate, perhaps at Davenham. His younger brother, George, was curate under his father at Mobberley. By 1635 Thomas Mallory junior had acquired a wife, Jane, and children, one of whom, Francis, was bequeathed 20 guineas, a very substantial sum, by Bishop Forster. But the curate installed at Northenden in 1616, a Mobberley man called Ralph Lowndes, still lived at the parsonage in Northenden. Thomas Mallory came to Northenden in 1640 after the death of Ralph Lowndes. By then his first wife had died and he had married Mary. So at the time of the siege Mallory was very much a newcomer to his parish.

His presence in the garrison was probably one of necessity, as well as conviction. He was ejected from the parsonage by the Parliamentarians in September 1643, at the same time as Tatton's step-father, Dr Nicholls, was ejected from the living of Cheadle.[15] Mrs Mary Mallory and her large family were allowed to remain in the parsonage, unmolested by the Parliamentarians, at least until the arrival of Henry Dunster in 1645, when she retired to the small cottage that was part of the glebe lands, all the time drawing a fifth of her husband's stipend and farming part of the glebe lands.

The parochial gentry numbered five in the garrison (Mr Mallory can also be considered a member of this group), including the two Twyfords, Henry Pendleton, the son and grandson of Manchester cloth merchants, and Richard Vawdrey of Bank Hall, Bowdon. The two latter were not local to Wythenshawe. Henry Pendleton lived in Manchester, where he owned property worth £800. Like the Carter brothers, he was a refugee from the siege. In 1648 he compounded for his delinquency and regained his estates for a fine of £80.

Richard Vawdrey's presence in the garrison is interesting because, like Mallory, he could have been there from necessity as well as conviction. He was Roman Catholic. Tatton may have been reluctant to admit Vawdrey to his garrison at first, but the man did come of a large and powerful local family. His younger brother, William, was also Roman Catholic, but most of the rest of the family were staunch Parliamentarians. Richard Vawdrey was also brother to one of Robert Tatton's close neighbours and friends, Henry Vawdrey of Hazelhurst in Baguley. Richard ended his days in the 1660s as master of Hazelhurst, after the death of his brother.

Most of the Vawdrey family living in Altrincham, Bowdon, Hale, Timperley, Sale and Baguley in the 1630s were the grandchildren and great-grandchildren of one man, Robert Vawdrey, Vice-chamberlain of the County Palatine of Chester during the reigns of Henry VIII, Edward VI, Mary Tudor and Elizabeth I. Richard, Henry and the Vawdreys of Riddings, Timperley, were the descendants of his first marriage. The descendants of his second marriage included a mayor of the nearby town of Altrincham. Henry, Richard and William were the sons of John, second and favourite son of Robert Vawdrey. Robert Vawdrey of the Riddings, agent of the Court of Wards in the 1630s, and his sister, Rebecca, the wife of Henry Cockson, Robert Tatton's manor steward, were the grandchildren of Thomas, the eldest son. Richard, John's eldest son, inherited Bank Hall. Henry, the second son inherited Hazelhurst from his mother, and William, by marrying the young heiress, Mary Massey, daughter and co-heir of John Massey of Ollerbarrow Hall in Hale, gained substantial property in that township.[16]

After the First Civil War Richard Vawdrey was charged with delinquency. Because he was a Catholic and owned lands worth over £200, he was threatened with imprisonment and confiscation of his estates. Only the prompt action of his Protestant brother, Henry, saved Richard. Henry Vawdrey convinced the Sequestrators that Richard had given him Bank Hall before the

Civil War and promised that his brother would not fight for the King again. Fortunately Henry Vawdrey was dealing with the Bucklow sequestrators and not their more zealous counterparts in Macclesfield Hundred.

The last and smallest group in the garrison were the country elite, the two esquires, Edward Legh and, of course, Robert Tatton, whose social status and families have been discussed elsewhere.

The average age of those members of the garrison who can be traced through parish registers (twenty-three out of the fifty-two), was just over thirty. This does include the ages of three young boys, Henry Coppocke, fifteen, Thomas Bailey, eight, and Robert Grantham, twelve. The oldest, at fifty-nine, was James Renshawe. It was probably Renshawe and his son, Robert, who, together with another man who was not named as a member of the garrison, William Smith, accompanied Tatton to Chester as soldier/servants. They were listed in 1648 as delinquents and William Smith was fined £1 because he had freehold land worth £10 a year. In a lease dated October 1650, in which Robert Renshawe took over his deceased father's land, the normal entry fine was waived by Robert Tatton "in consideracon of Service all ready done him by the said Robert Rainshaw".[17]

The fifty-two men of the garrison were not the only occupants of Wythenshawe Hall during those hard months of the siege. Mistress Anne Tatton, her six young children, and some female servants were also there, and it is not unreasonable to think that Robert Tatton might have offered safe refuge to his two sisters and their children whilst their husbands were in the garrison. The total in the hall could have been between eighty and ninety people, amongst them nine young children under the age of ten. The chaos of armed men, weapons, gunpowder and several lively, curious children, as well as Eleanor Legh in the first stages of her fifth pregnancy, all confined in one not over large house, a few outbuildings and stables, must have been horrendous.

Royalists, Parliamentarians or Apathetic Neutrals – the allegiances of the copyhold tenants in Northenden and Etchells

Only twenty members of the Wythenshawe Garrison were copyhold tenants from either Northenden or Etchells. Twenty out of 150 tenants does not seem to be a very large proportion. Why was this so?

It could be that Parliament had a greater influence in the two manors than the lord of the manor. Copyholders and yeomen freeholders were more often attracted to Parliament's side than to the King's. Parliament's stand against taxation without its approval and a more Puritan type of worship in the churches, appealed to those most affected by taxation – the copyholders and freeholders. There are known to have been a number of Parliamentarians and Puritans amongst the copyholders and freeholders of Northenden and Etchells, Captain Edmund Shelmerdine of Kenworthy, Francis Shelmerdine of Chamber Hall, curate of Cheadle, Richard But-

ton of Northern Moor and Henry Cockson of Kenworthy, lawyer, steward of the manor courts and kinsman to Robert Tatton. These prominent local Parliamentarians will be discussed more fully in Chapter 4. They were well-known local men with probably a great deal of influence, although at the moment, their exact influence cannot be measured in numbers, as it can be for Robert Tatton.

Seventeenth century JPs thought alehouses the hotbeds of rebellion and religious dissention. Attempts were made in some parts of the country to control alehouses with licences. In the late sixteenth century Cheshire had fifty-four inns, and 390 alehouses (one alehouse to fifty-one inhabitants).[18] There were four permanent alehouses in Northenden, run by the Deans, the Coppocks, the Barlows and Randle Hollinworth, the blacksmith. Only one was run by a family known to have Royalist sympathies, James Dean at the Boat House. There were three alehouses in Etchells, the Blomeleys of Gatley, the Heyes and the Baileys of Shadow Moss. There was probably also an alehouse or inn at Moss Nook (on the north-eastern edge of Shadow Moss), called Tatton House, held by George Linney.[19] The Blomeleys of Gatley had Royalist sympathies. In all there were nine alehouses serving a population of 600 people, sixty-six people (including women and children) to every alehouse. This seems to be slightly above the county average but in practice was probably more than enough for the two manors.

What evidence is there that the alehouses in Northenden and Etchells were used to spread rebellion and sedition? Very little. In fact the only example comes from the Restoration in 1662 when Edmund Shelmerdine, ex-Parliamentarian army officer, spoke out in a Northenden alehouse against the gentry and wished that they had all been murdered as in Germany.[20]

It might be expected from the above that most of the copyholders were Parliamentarian, turning against their landlord. But there is evidence that this was not the case. In 1644 Captain Edmund Shelmerdine had to take soldiers with him to collect rents from the copyholders, which he would hardly need to do if the latter were sympathetic to Parliament.

There is some slight evidence of the influence of Parliament in Northenden, although it is more of religious than a political nature (religion and politics were inseparable in the seventeenth century).

Probably the picture we should have is that some of the tenants were sympathetic to their landlord, some sympathetic to Parliament, but the great mass of people had little interest in the ideology of either beyond what affected them personally. Some local freeholders and tenants showed their support for Robert Tatton by supplying him with arms and food (more on them in the next chapter).

When Robert's neighbour, William Davenport of Bramhall Hall, tried to recruit his tenants for the King in September 1642 they presented a petition to him.

'Howsoever wee would not for the world harbour a disloyall thought against his Majestie yett wee dare not lifte upp our handes

9

against that honourable assembly off Parlament, whom we are conffydently assured doe labour both for the happiness of his Majestie and all his kingdome.'

At least one of those who signed his name to the above documents joined the Parliamentarian army.[21]

One reason for the apparent apathy was that to join Tatton's garrison or the Parliamentarians the tenants would have to stop working their own land during the time of ploughing, planting or harvesting or from working at their crafts. The 1630s had been a time of depression, especially for those in the clothing trades, so people could not afford to leave their ways of making a living for some unspecified length of time. Their families would suffer great hardship, even more so if the husband was killed in battle or siege.

Having said that, it is very surprising just how many families, fathers, sons and brothers, joined Robert Tatton's garrison. There were four families from Northenden and Etchells in the garrison, a total of ten people in all.

Another reason could be that although the most of the tenants were broadly sympathetic to Robert Tatton and the Royalist cause, like Royalist sympathisers in the rest of Cheshire, especially those in Chester, until 1645 they assumed that the King would win through Divine Right. He had God on his side. The strength and determination of the Parliamentarian rebellion was not truly realised until the second battle of Nantwich in 1644 when the Parliamentarian General Sir Thomas Fairfax roundly defeated Lord John Byron and forced him to retreat to Chester. By the time the Royalists realised their mistake it was too late. The county was already in the strong grip of Parliamentarians like General Sir William Brereton and Sir George Booth of Dunham.

Notes

1. E. Broxap, *The Great Rebellion in Lancashire*, p.18, p.40, Manchester University Press, 1910.
2. G. Ormerod, editor, 'Civil War Tracts of Lancashire', *Chetham Society*, OS, Vol 2, p.43.
3. R.N. Dore, '*The Great Civil War in The Manchester Area*', p.14.
4. Robert Tatton's Delinquency Papers in the Public Record Office, quoted in Earwaker, Vol 1.
5. Robert Tatton's Delinquency Papers in the Public Record Office, quoted in Earwaker, Vol 1, p.302.
6. *Cheshire 1630-1660*, p.133.
7. Earwaker, Vol 1.
8. For a very full account of the Bretland Case see R.N. Dore and J.S. Morrill, 'The Allegiance of the Cheshire Gentry', Appendix B, *Transactions of the Lancashire and Cheshire Antiquarian Society* (TLCAS), Vol 77.
9. J Ry L Tatton Family Papers, the deposition of James Brownhill, taken before the Sequestration Committee for Macclesfield Hundred and dated 30th October, 1646; Calendar for the Proceedings of the Committee for Compounding (CPCC) – William Smith compounded in 1651 when he confessed that he was made prisoner after the siege of Wythenshawe Hall in 1644.
10. R.N. Dore, editor, *The Letter Books of Sir William Brereton*', LCRS, Vol I, (Vol 123 in LCRS series), item no.385.
11. The Protestation Returns of Didsbury, February, 1642.
12. Ormerod, Vol 1, p.421.
13. Christopher Hill, *Century of Revolution*.
14. Earwaker, Vol 1, pp.292-3.
15. Ibid.
16. A.C. Matthews, *Walker Revised: Being a Revision of John Walker's Sufferings of the Clergy During the Grand Rebellion 1642-1660*, Oxford University Press, 1948, p.92; Ormerod, Vol II; Tatton Family Pedigree, Earwaker, Vol 1.
17. Both Ollerbarrow and Bank Hall were rebuilt in the 18th century and still survive, the latter as a riding stables, the former, once a police station, a WRVS post and now an antique shop. For his second wife William Vawdrey married Alice, the daughter of Edward Moore of Thelwall, a noted Parliamentarian.
18. BL Harleian Mss 2130 quoted in Earwaker, Vol 1; Ormerod Vol 1; J Ry L Tatton Family Papers, lease no. 986.
19. Parish Register of St James Didsbury, 1561-1757, Vol 1, Part 1, published by the Lancashire Parish Register Society; the first volume of the Northenden Parish Register, as yet unpublished.
20. Peter Clark, *The English Alehouse: A Social History, 1200-1830*, p.42.
21. J Ry L Tatton Family Papers, no. 339, the Court Leet Records of Northenden 1667 – 1700; the Court Leet Records of Etchells 1660-1730; Tatton Family Papers, no. 341, Rental Survey 1670.
22. J.H. Hodson, *Cheshire 1660 to 1780: Restoration to Industrial Revolution*, Vol 9 in the Cheshire History Series.
23. Earwaker, Vol 1, pp.429-30, a letter dated September 17th, 1642.

The Siege of Wythenshawe Hall

Events in Cheshire, January 1643 – February 1644

On January 27th Sir William Brereton and Sir Thomas Aston met in battle at Nantwich. Both leaders had raw troops, many of whom did not know one end of a pike or musket from the other. The battle was decided in Brereton's favour when one of his men had the bright idea of firing a small drake (little cannon),causing the Royalists to flee in alarm.[1]

In the same month some 'Manchester Men' made an attempt to storm Adlington Hall but returned without accomplishing anything.[2] News of this probably made Robert Tatton increase the speed of his own siege preparations.

A few weeks later the battle of Middlewich took place. Like the first battle of Nantwich, two inexperienced forces were pitted against each other and it was largely a matter of luck that Brereton won again. For the second time in as many months Aston returned to Chester without his men. Shortly afterwards he was recalled to Oxford. Less than a year later he died of wounds received in battle.

Most of Cheshire gradually fell under Brereton's control, partly aided by the collapse of Lord Derby's power in the shambles at Sabden Brook, near Blackburn. Then Stafford and the supposedly impregnable fortress of Beeston Castle near Chester fell, giving Brereton control of the Midland Gap, the marching route of any large army coming up from the south. Warrington fell to Colonel John Booth (second son of Sir George Booth) in May, giving the Parliamentarians control of all the bridges over the River Mersey between it and Stockport (a distance of some twenty miles or more).

All this was achieved in Cheshire at a time when Parliament was retreating before the Royalists in the rest of the country. Why was this Parliamentarian victory possible in Cheshire and Lancashire? Two major reasons accounted for it. Firstly, for most of 1643 the King only saw the two counties as troop fodder and, secondly, many Royalists in Cheshire supported a concentration of the county's resources on Chester. In the autumn of 1643 Brereton began to cut off Chester's Welsh supplies.

The King, now aware of Chester's importance as the chief disembarking port for the Earl of Ormonde's troops from Ireland, decided something must be done. Between November 21st and 24th twenty Irish and West Country ships landed 4,000 infantry at Mostyn in Flintshire. Brereton's Lancashire troops, fearing Liverpool might be their true objective, returned home, leaving Brereton with no choice but to retreat.

In mid-December the Royalist commander, Lord Byron, arrived from Oxford with a thousand cavalry. Beeston, Hawarden and Wrexham were re-taken. Byron began harassing Nantwich with raids, capturing Major Lothian, the military advisor to Sir George Booth, governor of the garrison. On Christmas Day Byron attacked Brereton at Middlewich, a defeat in which the latter lost 500 men at least.

However, help was on the way in the form of the Yorkshire General, Sir Thomas Fairfax, together with 1,800 cavalry. Without him Nantwich would have fallen and the Parliamentarian cause in Cheshire and Lancashire have been lost.

Byron and Fairfax met in battle outside Nantwich on the morning of January 25th. The numbers on both sides were evenly matched. So it was the entry of the Nantwich garrison into the fray, who had no knowledge of Fairfax's presence until they heard the fighting, that decided the day in favour of the Parliamentarians.

Casualties were light but the victory decisive. It made Parliament's dominance in Lancashire and Cheshire all but complete. Apart from Chester, Royalist resistance was now confined in small pockets – Crewe Hall, Doddington Hall and Lathom Hall (held by the Countess of Derby) in Lancashire, Adlington and Wythenshawe in Cheshire. With the exception of Lathom Hall, all of these fell to Fairfax within a month of the victory at Nantwich.[3]

Sir Thomas Fairfax left Cheshire in April 1644. A year later he became Commander-in-Chief of the New Model Army with the then relatively unknown Oliver Cromwell as his General of Cavalry.

Supplies for the Wythenshawe Garrison

Any garrison, whether in a small hall, a large town or a castle, needs two kinds of supplies to withstand a siege – food and arms. Most of the primary evidence for both food and arms supplies at Wythenshawe comes from the inventory taken sometime between February and June 1644. The dating of this inventory has caused some confusion. It is endorsed on the back 'taken away from Robert Tatton of Withinshawe in the yeare 1643 by Thomas Fairfax, Coronale Duckenfield and others, Commanders in Cheefe'. There is a further date added, June 19 Caroli. These two dates caused the eminent nineteenth century Cheshire historian, J.P. Earwaker, and the writers of 'Wythenshawe: Vol 1 to 1926' to give the inventory the highly improbable date of June 1643 when Fairfax was still on the eastern side of the Pennines and Robert Tatton not yet under siege. They did not realise that in the seventeenth century a new year did not begin officially until March 25th and so misinterpreted the '19 Caroli'. The true date of this inventory is probably June 1644 and it is likely to be a fair copy of a list of the contents of the hall made immediately after the surrender in February 1644, hence the date 1643. '19 Caroli' refers to the nineteenth year of King Charles's reign, which was 1644. (Fair copies of probate inventories were often given the dates of the original rough copies.)

Towards the end of the inventory there is a very detailed list of the arms found in the hall.

'Armes in the House.

Item. The Ensigne.

Item. One large Drume with Mr. Tatton's Coate of Armes & three

other Drummes.
Item. Two Holberts.
Item. One compliate lance.
Item. Sixe Cosletts with Head peece & Swords.
Item. Three Head peeces for Musketeers.
Item. Twenty two Pikes.
Item. Thirty two Musketts with Bandileers & Rests.
Item. Foure longe fowling Pieces.
Item. Sixe lesser Pieces.
Item. Two Carbines & one Calliver.
Item. Foure Cases of Pistolls with Holsters.
Item. Bills Pole Axes & halfe Pykes 12.
Item. A steele rack Bowe & a steele Crosse Bowe.
Item. Eight longe Bowes & 2 quiver of Arrowes of 5 dozen.
Item. A Hundred weight of Powder with Matche & Bullets answerable.[4]

This gives a total of ninety-eight weapons, just less than two per member of the garrison. Each man had a weapon for distance fighting (a musket or a long bow) and a weapon for hand-to-hand fighting (a pike or a bill).

It might seem surprising that in 1643 long bows and cross bows were still in use. After all they were no longer the mainstay of an English army. Long bows were last used as such during the reign of Henry VIII. So were these eight long bows belonging grandfathers, taken out of a dark corner and dusted off? Definitely not. A long bow was a very perishable commodity. The bows were certainly less than ten years old and the strings new, probably less than a year. The inventory of Henry Legh, father of Edward, mentions a long bow, so perhaps one of the bows came from Baguley Hall.[5]

What would have been the use of such antiquated weapons when muskets were coming into greater use in European and English armies? There are three reasons for the presence of long bows in Wythenshawe Hall. Firstly, they were good hunting weapons. Secondly, it would be a matter of pride for a Cheshireman to be a proficient marksman at the Sunday butts. After all Cheshire provided most of the archers who stood against the French in the mud at Crecy, Poitiers and Agincourt. The Court Leet/Court Baron of Etchells records the presence of the 'Shooting Butts' and the need to keep them in good repair even in the late seventeenth century.

The third reason is a practical one. An experienced archer, drawing a bow of 90lb weight, could kill a man at 200 yards and seriously maim him at 300 yards. With the right type of arrow, that would apply even to a man in armour. Muskets, and even rifles, were only accurate to less than 100 yards, pistols less than 50 yards. Long bows also had the advantage of rapid loosing, one arrow every ten seconds if need be. A musketeer could only manage to fire once a minute.

The inventory mentions 'A steele rack Bowe & a steel Crosse Bowe'. These were probably two types of cross bow. The 'steele rack Bowe' would refer to the heavy, military crossbow, usually known as an arbalest, which was strained by a small windlass or rack until it reached the right tension for firing. The other was probably a lighter hunting crossbow, very popular in England in the reign of Elizabeth I. It was bent back by a goat's foot lever. The arbalest is an unusual find in an English household. Popular in Europe during the fifteenth century, by the seventeenth century it had been largely superceded by the musket. Perhaps Robert Tatton's great-grandfather had bought it and the quarrels to go with it as a mild curiosity, a different weapon to use in hunting, or perhaps it was brought to the garrison by a friend.[6]

Like the long bows, both types of crossbow had great accuracy over long distances, though not quite as far as the long bow – 150 yards.

The muskets used by the Wythenshawe garrison were probably of the smooth bore, improved matchlock type. The 'Foure long fowlinge Pieces', as their description suggests, were not military guns but sporting rifles. They were fitted with doglocks or snaphaunces (primitive flintlocks). Often elaborately decorated on the lock and along the length of the barrel, which could be anything between five and six feet (the longer the barrel the greater the accuracy it was thought), these fowling pieces were very popular with the gentry and aristocracy in the seventeenth and eighteenth centuries.

Lesser fowling pieces, with barrels of only four-foot, were distinguished by the slight flare of the muzzle and ornamental mouldings.[7]

Carbines were heavy cavalry weapons, three-and-a-half feet in length, generally snaphaunces and lighter than muskets, carried slung from the shoulder or belt by a swivel. The calliver was a lighter version of the musket. By 1643 they were slightly old-fashioned weapons, because they used shot too light to pierce armour. One or two Civil War military historians had thought that the calliver was no longer use in the 1640s – until they were told about the Wythenshawe inventory.

The 'Foure cases of Pistolls with Holsters' were probably cavalry pistols, perhaps even 'turned-off' pistols, hard-hitting, short range weapons. The barrel was unscrewed at the breach so that a heavy charge and ball could be put into the chamber, the walls of which were specially thickened to withstand the explosion of the discharge. These pistols were designed to penetrate heavy armour and were full-length cavalry weapons. They disappeared after the Restoration.

The bills, pikes, pole-axes and halberts were standard sixteenth and seventeenth century infantry weapons for close hand-to-hand fighting. The ensign, of course, was a flag, perhaps, like the drum, bearing the Tatton arms. The four drums would probably be played by the youngest members of the garrison, Thomas Bailey, Robert Grantham, Henry Coppock and Henry Renshawe.

A closer inspection of this list of weapons makes it possible to see a clear division between the weapons for the ordinary soldiers – pikes, bows and muskets – and those for the gentry – swords, half-pikes, fowling pieces, pistols and carbines.

Where did all these weapons come from? Obviously some came from Wythenshawe itself, the fowling pieces, the armour and perhaps the cross bows. Some came from neighbours and supporters. One delivery was the occasion of a small accident. 'Mr. Thomas Gerard of the Riddings came into the Garrison at Withinshawe, his pistol exploded and shot him in the thigh.'[8] Perhaps he brought the cavalry pistols.

However, the majority of the arms, the muskets, the pikes, the drums, the gunpowder, the flag, were official military arms. The Trained Band for Macclesfield Hundred joined Sir William Brereton. However, it is likely that Tatton, who was a captain of the band, would have stored these arms in his house. According to the 1609 'Boke of Ye Trayned Bands', of Cheshire (found amongst the Tatton Family Papers) the townships of Northenden and Etchells should have produced three corsletts, two muskets, two callivers and seven men. The total complement of muskets for Macclesfield Hundred was thirty.[9] Robert Tatton had thirty-two in 1644. On the other hand, it is possible that, like Sir Edward Fitton and Thomas Legh, Robert Tatton confiscated arms from the Parliamentarians amongst his tenants.

Why did Robert Tatton, even as an officer in the Trained Band, have such ready access to its arms? The reason is that Tatton obtained the arms through his tenants. According to five leases granted in the 1630s, two wills and two inventories in return for reducing the boons and services on tenements with rents above a certain amount, some tenants were to provide, at their own cost, Trained Band weapons, such as muskets, corslets and pikes. The wording used in the leases confirms that these were Trained Band weapons and that Robert Tatton was a Trained Band captain trying to modernise his company's equipment in the 1630s. The tenants were to have the weapons:-

'ready to serve our sourigne lord the kings Ma:tie his highnes heires & successors in the time of warres & trouble soe often as the said Rob[er]t Tatton his heires or assignes shalbee appointed or commanded to serve or show his armes in anywise'.

Only these 1630s leases amongst all the hundreds of Tatton leases have this additional tenant duty or obligation, but three early eighteenth century surveys and rentals of the Booth family's large estates in Cheshire and Lancashire show that they could raise a total of 475 armed men (the equivalent to a Trained Band regiment) equipped with muskets, halberts, bills, pikes and corslets. The arms mentioned in the survey and rental are slightly old-fashioned for the early eighteenth century an perhaps represent something which was begun in the 1630s, as Robert Tatton had done with his tenants. On the other hand, perhaps this duty was begun at the time of the Monmouth Rebellion in 1684 or the Glorious Revolution in 1688, in both of which Henry Booth (son of young Colonel George) was heavily involved.[10]

Although the weapons were bought by the tenants at the instigation of Robert Tatton, they were considered the tenant's property by probate appraisors. Robert Miller owned a sword, a pike and gorget worth a total of 10s in 1642. John Cockson of Sharston Green owned an old sword in 1670 which he probably used during the siege of Wythenshawe Hall in 1644 (it must have been a good quality of sword to have survived thirty years – most swords issued to ordinary soldiers of either side were very poor quality and frequently did not survive one battle).[11]

Pikes, bills, gorgets, corslets and swords could have been made by the local blacksmiths, Randle Hollinworth and Arnold Watts. But the muskets were made by gunsmiths. Northenden had a craftsman who called himself a gunsmith in the late seventeenth century, Richard Goulden, who, when younger styled himself a whitesmith (someone who finished goods). Matchlock muskets were smooth bore and had simple trigger mechanisms which could easily be made by a whitesmith. Now Richard Goulden's will shows that he was a Calvinist Presbyterian (he must have been one of the last in Northenden when he died at the age of eighty in 1700). He should have had Parliamentarian sympathies, but he had strong family connections with the Tattons in the second half of the seventeenth century. His eldest son, Aaron, became a servant to Thomas Tatton, Robert's third son. He was a friend of Ellen Coppock, who was probably a servant to the Tattons before she married Robert Coppock (a younger brother of the fifteen year old Henry Coppock who was a member of the garrison). Richard Goulden was a pillar of Northenden society in the late seventeenth century and was called in by the court leet to give evidence on local customs on quite a few occasions.[12]

Food was as important as weapons. How much and what sort of food was in Wythenshawe Hall? That is not easy to answer. What is noted in the inventory is the little left at the end of the siege. In the case of preserved food and drink stored in barrels it is possible to roughly estimate the quantities.

In the Store House	£	s	d
Item. Two great Beefe Tubbes	3	10	0
Item. Two great Butter Tubbes	2	00	0
Item. Fourteene Beare Barrells	6	00	0
Item. Two little Beefe Tubbes	0	13	4
Item. Three little Butter Tubbes	0	08	0
Item. Sixe Firkins	0	12	0
Item. Two Wine Barrels	0	01	0
In the Garner			
Item. Windowed oates eight bushells & a half	8	14	0
Item. Tenn bushells & three Hoopes of towle corn	8	00	0
Item. Seaven bushells of Shillinge	5	12	0
Item. An ould bushell of Wheate	1	06	8
Item. Three Bushells of Pease & Beanes	3	06	0
Item. Foure Bushells of latter end of Oates	2	13	4
Item. Twelve Bushells of Dust	0	16	0
Sum	30	08	0'[13]

The 'Two great Beefe Tubbes' were tubs of beef salted down,for winter as siege supplies. They had an approximate capacity of over 100 gallons each. These together with the 'Two little Beefe Tubbes' (probably the same size as the beer barrels – 36 gallons each), would be enough for the Tatton household of twenty to thirty people during the winter. During the siege this salt beef (the equivalent of four or five beef carcasses) would have to feed upwards of eighty people for over three months.

The 'Two great Butter Tubbes' were probably the same size as the beef tubs, though worth 15s less, and the 'Three little Butter Tubbes' were probably firkin size (nine gallons). The contents of the butter tubs would have been put down with layers of salt in the summer and autumn months when the grass would be at its best and the milk creamier. Cheese was also made at the same time. There was a dairy equipped to make cheese as well as butter attached to Wythenshawe Hall (Cheshire cheese was the county's oldest, most valuable and well-known export). However, there was a tradition in Cheshire in the seventeenth century of making some butter from the whey. Ten ounces of butter per cow per week could be made in this way. This was the ordinary, everyday butter made and used immediately when the cows were in milk, not the butter salted down for winter use when the cows were dry.

Cheese, along with bacon, oat cakes and maslin bread, was more the normal daily fare for the people of Northenden and Etchells in the mid-seventeenth century than salt beef.[14] The inventory gives no indication of how much cheese had been in the hall but probably as much as six hundredweight had been consumed between late November 1643 and late February, 1644. It could be that as many as ten pigs were salted and smoked into bacon and eaten during the siege (although there is no mention of the swine turnells or troughs in which the sides of bacon were salted, in the inventory).

The beer in the fourteen barrels was brewed either by Robert Tatton himself or the household steward. It was a matter of pride in the seventeenth century for a gentleman to brew his own beer (or at least oversee the brewing of it). Robert was building a new brewhouse in brick when the Civil War errupted.[15] In a cold storehouse the beer would have kept for up to six months – if allowed to.

Assuming the six firkins were once full of beer, together with the barrels, there would have been 554 gallons of beer in the storehouse. It sounds a great deal but it was only enough to provide a pint each day for the garrison. The two small wine barrels were two or three gallon casks and only for the consumption of Robert Tatton, his family and the other gentry. There was also water from the well.

It is difficult to guess how much was in the garner when the siege began. What was left at the end, according to the inventory, was less than a week's food for both people and animals (there were several horses in the stables and other livestock to feed). In November 1643 the garner might have been full with over 100 bushells each of wheat, oats, towle corn, peas, beans and shilling (malted barley roasted in the kiln and waiting to be milled for brewing).

Most of the food came from the demesne lands of Wythenshawe and Peele – over 210 acres. There is also evidence that some of Robert's friends and neighbours, whilst not so committed to the Royalist cause as he, sympathised enough to send gifts of food.

'the s[ai]d Mr. Gerrard associated himself w[i]th the s[ai]d Mr. Tatton, and sent either malt or wheat to this dep[onen]ts knowledge in a Jack towards the menteyance of the s[ai]d Garrison.'

'Roger Worthington of Crosse Acres in the Towne[shi]pp of Etchells...did associate himselfe w[i]th the said Mr. Tatton and sent wheat to the s[ai]d Mr. Tatton towards the menteyance of the s[ai]d Garrison.'[16]

These were more gestures of support than attempts to feed the whole garrison.

Intelligence Gathering for the Wythenshawe Garrison

Robert Tatton had supporters who counselled him, gave him arms, food and probably news, but did not join the garrison itself. Amongst those most frequently named by witnesses were Thomas Gerrard of the Riddings, Henry Vawdrey, William Davenport of Baguley, Roger Worthington of Cross Acres and Robert Hollinprist of Hale. These gentlemen often visited Robert at night as well as during the day time and had secret conferences with him in the Banqueting House.

'And this dep[onen]t further saith That hee hath oftene seene Mr. William Davenport of Baguley in the s[ai]d garrison severall tymes only in the night and did Associate and had private Conference w[i]th the s[ai]d Mr. Tatton att the s[ai]d Banqueting-house.'[17]

Thomas Gerrard was living at Riddings Hall, Timperley, either with Robert Vawdrey, to whom he was related by marriage, or tenanting it, or part of it. Later, in 1659, Thomas Gerrard was to give evidence against Dr Peter Harrison, the rector of Cheadle, for his part in young Sir George Booth's Rising, a turnaround for one who had supported a Royalist in the First Civil War. In 1660 he bought Riddings Hall from his impoverished landlord.

William Davenport of Baguley was a member of the parochical gentry and came of a very junior branch of either the Davenports of Bramhall. Very little is known of him or his family. In 1616, when William Davenport was born, his father, also William Davenport, was described as being of Hazelhurst (Henry Vawdrey's residence). The first William Davenport's mother was Avis Vawdrey, the widow of Thomas Vawdrey of Riddings (therefore Robert Vawdrey's grandmother), Henry's uncle. For her second husband she married Humphrey Davenport, so it is quite possible that for a time her son resided at Hazelhurst.[18]

What sort of aid and advice did William Davenport give Robert Tatton? Did he collect intelligence on the enemy's movements, such as the attempt on Adlington by the 'Manchester Men' and the defeat of the Royalists at Nantwich and Middlewich?

Roger Worthington of Cross Acres was a substantial tenant of Robert Tatton's, tenanting 28 acres in Etchells and perhaps had a good few acres freehold in Cross Acres.[19] Of Robert Hollinprist of Hale nothing is known. Perhaps he was a freeholder with a farm in Hale Low, now part of Altrincham.

So, just as Robert Tatton drew most of his committed support for the garrison from the parochical gentry/yeomanry, so he drew most of his uncommitted support for supplies and intelligence from the same social group.

The Siege of Wythenshawe, November 21st 1643 – February 27th, 1644

On November 21st, 1643 the long-waited Parliamentarian assault on Wythenshawe Hall was begun by a cap-

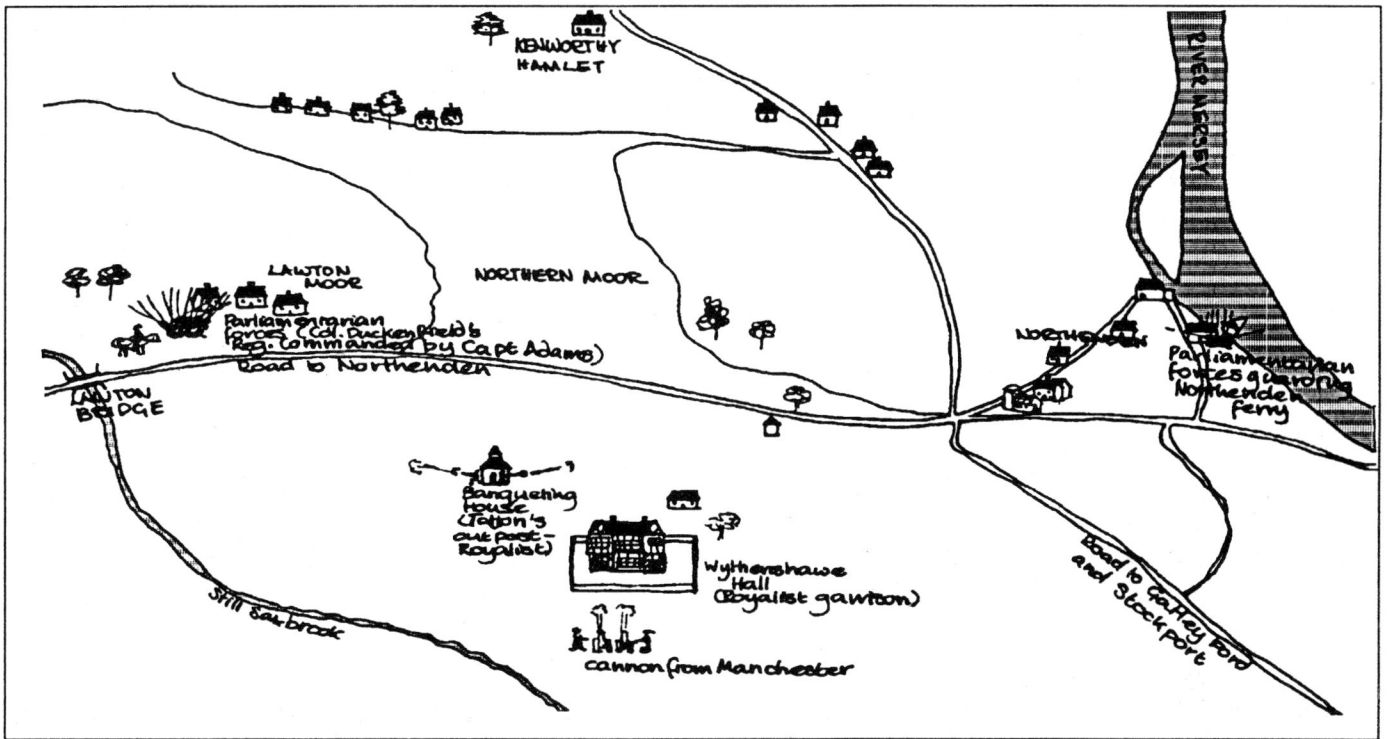

Siege of Wythenshawe Hall. November 25th, 1643 – February 27th 1644. Possible troop depositions. North is the top of the map. Distance about a mile from top to bottom and three miles from left to right.

tain and thirty men of Colonel Robert Duckenfield 's regiment. It took them over three months and two cannon brought from Manchester to reduce the hall. Wythenshawe surrendered on February 27th, 1644 and its some of its garrison imprisoned at Stockport.[20] Robert was allowed to travel to the Royalist city of Chester. His brother-in-law, Edward Legh, his pregnant wife, Eleanor, and their children also went to Chester at the same time.

Why did it take so long to reduce a small, half-timbered hall, garrisoned by inexperienced men? There are several reasons for this:-

1. November was not a good month in which to begin a siege, being very cold and wet. Often the first heavy snows of winter would fall in November (the seventeenth century was a mini ice-age) and seriously hamper troop movement. The soldiers' gun-match would often be too damp to fire the muskets. Then there was the demoralising misery of bivouacking out in the snow or in some poor tenants' hovel in nearby Lawton or Northern Moor, cold and shivering, knowing that their adversaries were warmer, their gun-match drier and their bellies better filled. The worst of the weather of the winter of 1643/44 occurred between Christmas and the end of January, when there were heavy, lingering falls of snow. The second battle of Nantwich was fought over snow-covered ground.

2. It is more than likely that Colonel Robert Duckenfield himself was never present at the siege of Wythenshawe Hall. The majority of his regiment took part with Brereton in the relief of Nantwich. Without the strict, if a little young and inexperienced, eye of their

colonel the troops might not set about a winter siege with the vigour and determination it needed. Some of the men would have been recruited from neighbouring areas to the east, if not in Northenden and Etchells themselves (Edmund Shelmerdine of Kenworthy was a captain in Duckenfield's regiment and the captain of this small troop, Adams, was a Stockport man) and the temptation to return home and visit wives and families must have been nigh impossible to resist.

3. Wythenshawe Hall was defended by a moat and a low retaining wall, and it had a forward outpost in the shape of the little wooden Banqueting House (fashionable in the seventeenth century for serving the 'banqueting' course at a feast). During the heavy snows Robert Tatton could easily put ten or twenty men in there and keep them replenished with ammunition and food. From there they could ambush Duckenfield's troops or sally out to skirmish with them.[21]

4. Duckenfield's men had some experience of battle, but they were not yet the crack troops they were to become in the 'Leaguer' of Chester and the battle of Worcester in 1651, nor were they well-versed in siege warfare. Duckenfield himself was a very young colonel of just twenty-four in 1643.

   All the sources on the siege of Wythenshawe Hall agree that there were thirty troops under Captain Adams. Thirty was a very small number for even a captain's company, about half the usual full company compliment. Edmund Shelmerdine commanded a company of about sixty men in 1645.

   It is a well-known law in siege warfare that if an attacking force wants to take a city or a castle quickly it must be at least twice the size of the garrison. Captain Adam's force was only just over half the size of Tatton's – what Brereton could spare whilst the rest of the Cheshire Parliamentarian forces were trying to combat and contain Byron with his Irish troops.

5. Captain Adams took the only option open to him, given the weather and the resources he had. He cut off Tatton's access to supplies and waited to starve out the garrison. He frequently attacked to wear down morale and resistance as well as the garrison's stock of ammunition.

From the small amount of information available on the positions of troops on both sides it seems that Captain Adams stationed his men on Lawton Moor. This gave him a commanding position over the only passable road between Northenden village and the rest of Cheshire (now known as Wythenshawe Road). He also put troops into the Boathouse (later the Boat Inn, but then an unlicensed alehouse), where James Dean had his ferry boat (Dean was a member of Robert Tatton's garrison). Although, there is no evidence for this, in order to complete his depositions Captain Adams probably stationed some men by Gatley Ford to prevent supplies and men coming into Wythenshawe Hall from both sides of the River Mersey. But perhaps he did not need men on Gatley Ford since in winter the river would have been often in full spate. However, the first heavy snows of winter fell in late November and put paid to any thought of sending to Manchester for cannon to reduce the hall.

What was Wythenshawe Hall like during those months of siege? The 1644 inventory gives a list of the furniture in each room, and it is clear from this that some pieces were not in their usual places. The Great Dining Room on the ground floor, whose windows faced east towards the low retaining wall but not over it, contained several virginals, harpiscords, stools, couches and tables, all items normally in the Little Dining Room above. The latter was bare of all furniture except for heavy presses used for storing yarn. It had a good view out over the retaining wall and moat, and beyond into the Swine Park and so was cleared for use by musketeers and bowmen, as it was where the most frequent attacks took place. Cannon balls hit that side of the hall (in the seventeenth century it was the rear of the hall, not the front as it is today). It is possible that Captain Adams was shot dead whilst he was commanding the cannonade on that side of the hall by a musketeer firing from the Little Dining Room.

If Sir Thomas Fairfax had not sent the two cannon from Manchester would Wythenshawe have taken longer to surrender? Probably not. The gunpowder and shot for the muskets and rifles left in the inventory was only enough for two or three sorties or two day's defence. There was only enough food for a week, perhaps less. Wythenshawe may have been on the point of surrender when the cannon arrived. A short cannonade, which did some slight damage to the hall near the Little Dining Room windows but caused no casualties, convinced Robert Tatton and the other gentlemen to surrender on February 25th, 1644, the day that someone shot Captain Adams.

The known casualty figures for both sides were slight. Duckenfield lost three men from his company, including Captain Adams. Robert Tatton reputedly lost six men during an attack, perhaps a skirmish around the Banqueting House. Who they were is not known and there are no mention of them in contemporary accounts. However, according to Earwaker, six skeletons were found in the eighteenth century in the courtyard garden at Wythenshawe and these were claimed to be the remains of the Royalist soldiers who fell during the siege, and whom the Parliamentarian attackers would not allow to be buried in Northenden churchyard.[22]

After the surrender Tatton tried to prevent three horses being commandeered by Colonel Duckenfield's men according to an entry in the inventory.

'One Nagge & two Mares being taken from Mr. Tatton by Violence.'.[23]

Notes

1. *The Civil Wars in Cheshire*, p.26.
2. *The Great Civil War in Lancashire*, p.62.
3. *The Civil Wars in Cheshire*, pp.23-38.
4. J Ry L Tatton Family Papers, 1644 Inventory of the contents of Wythenshawe Hall in February 1644, reprinted in 'Wythenshawe: Vol 1 to 1926', p.55-69.
5. The probate inventory of Henry Legh of Baguley, esquire, dated 1635, CCRO.
6. Colonel H.C.B. Rogers, *Weapons of the British Soldier*, (1960), pp.39-40.
7. *The Book of the Gun*, Hamlyn, p.87.
8. A deposition from the Tatton Composition Papers in the Public Record Office, copy in J Ry L Tatton Family Papers.
9. J Ry L Tatton Family papers, no. 282, 'The Boke of Ye Trayned Bandes of Cheshire', 1609.
10. J Ry L Tatton Family Papers, leases 1071-1073 and 1431-1432; Joyce Littler, 'A Commentary on the 1701 Estate Survey and the Rentals of 1704 and 1709 of Dunham Massey' (1992). I am grateful to Joyce for letting me look at this in one of its drafts.
11. The inventories of Robert Miller, dated 1642 and John Cockson of Sharston Green, dated 1677 (CCRO).
12. The Will and inventory of Richard Goulden of Northenden, gunsmith, dated 1700 (CCRO); the Will of Ellen Coppock, widow, of Northenden, 1680; the Will of Thomas Tatton, 1690; J Ry L Tatton Family Papers, Northenden Court Leet Records. Richard Goulden's third son, John, followed his father as a gunsmith, inheriting his tools.
13. J Ry L Tatton Family Papers, 1644 inventory.
14. Inventories of Northenden and Etchells, 1620 – 1700 (CCRO).
15. J Ry L Tatton Family Papers, 1644 inventory.
16. J Ry L Tatton Family Papers, both extracts from the deposition of James Brownhill (listed as a member of the Wythenshawe garrison and who was Tatton's stable boy) before the Macclesfield Sequestration Committee in October 1646.
17. J Ry L Tatton Family Papers, the deposition of James Brownhill.
18. Northenden Parish Register, Book 1.
19. J Ry L Tatton Family Papers, 1648 Rental Survey.
20 J. Hall, *Memorials of the Civil Wars in Cheshire*, LCRS, Vol 19.
21. J Ry L Tatton Family Papers, another deposition.
22. Earwaker, Vol 1.
23. J Ry L Tatton Family Papers, 1644 Inventory.

4

Surviving Under Parliamentarian Rule

The Parliamentarian Faction in Northenden and Etchells

Despite what was said in Chapter 2 about the 'apathy' or Royalist sympathies of the copyholders of Northenden and Etchells there was a small group of Parliamentarians from the two manors, who were probably locally influential, but who also had some wider influence.

Francis Shelmerdine, Puritan curate to Dr Nicholls at Cheadle, subtenanted land in Etchells, Chamber Hall (so-called because it was originally the mediaeval court house or 'camera' hall of the Steward of the manor of Etchells) from at least the 1630s onwards. The very detailed 1670 Rental Survey says that Francis Shelmerdine's tenement was an ancient one.[1]

Shelmerdine joined the regiment of Colonel Robert Duckenfield of Duckenfield Hall (near Stockport) as chaplain sometime late in 1642 or early 1643. Later he was chaplain for the regiment of Colonel Henry Bradshawe during the abortive campaign of Charles II in 1651.[2] By June 1651 he was vicar of Mottram-in-Longdendale.[3]

Between the expulsion of Dr Nicholls from Cheadle in September 1643 and June 1651 Francis was acting rector of Cheadle and occasional preacher at Northenden until the permanent appointment of the Reverend Henry Dunster in 1644.[4]

Edmund Shelmerdine was a freeholder with 14 Cheshire measure acres in Kenworthy, a small settlement in Northenden.[5] He seems to have have had some local influence prior to the Civil Wars. He served on the jury that heard the Inquisition Post Mortem on Humphrey Bulkeley of Cheadle, heir of Richard Bulkeley held at Northwich on October 9th, 1639, before four gentlemen, including Sir George Booth and Dr William Nicholls.[6] By 1645 Edmund was a captain in Colonel Duckenfield's regiment, possibly replacing the Captain Adams who was killed at the siege of Wythenshawe Hall. According to a list of Cheshire forces in the Letter Books of Sir William Brereton (item no. 385) dated April 30th, 1645, Captain Shelmerdine, together with another, Captain Siddal (one of William Davenport of Bramhall's tenants), commanded a country company of 120 foot soldiers.[7] How many of these were raised from amongst Robert Tatton's tenants is not known. However, these names appear on a list of pensioners of Duckenfield's regiment under his command in 1651, Thomas Massey of Gatley, Richard Button of Moorside, a Goodyeare and a Cooke.[8] On August 12th, 1644, in company with William Barrett and Richard Button, both Macclesfield Sequestrators (the former later becoming an Independent preacher with Samuel Eaton at Stockport), Captain Edmund Shelmerdine went to Bramhall Hall to take an inventory of William Davenport's goods to assess the latter's delinquency fine.

'On Monday following, being the 12th of the said month... there came to Bramhall William Barret, Captain Edmund Shelmerdine,

Richard Button, George Newton, Gerard Hayes, Robert Ridgway, John Wharmby, Will. Thomson my owne tenant, Daniel of the Lane, Will. Smith, commissioners deputed by the sequestrators to Macclesfield Hundred...searching every corner causing all boxes and chests to be opened which otherwise they threatened to break up, being in the meantime guarded with a company of musketeers who stood in the park and all about the house with their matches lighted.'[9]

Richard Button was the sequestration agent for Robert Tatton's estates, which must have somewhat galled the latter since Button was a copyholder with a tenement of 14 Cheshire measure acres in Northern Moor, Northenden.[10]

Another Parliamentarian from the two manors was Henry Cockson. He was kinsman to Robert Tatton, a lawyer, hereditary steward of the manor courts of Northenden and Etchells, and Solicitor for Sequestrations in Cheshire. In terms of outside influence he was the greatest of all the Parliamentarians from the two manors.

Cockson was the grandson or great-grandson of Henry Cockson of the Hough, Withington in Lancashire, Steward of the manor courts in 1591 and who married Mary Tatton in 1580 (Robert Tatton's great-great aunt). Henry Cockson the great-grandson tenanted 16 Cheshire measure acres in Kenworthy in the manor of Northenden. There was another Henry Cockson in the two manors, holding 23 Cheshire acres in Poundswick, a close kinsman and friend of Henry Cockson the Steward.

Henry Cockson the Steward had lands and a coal pit in Clifton, near Prestwich, a house in Manchester, lands in Chester, Hale and Baguley, as well as the tenement in Kenworthy. How much of these lands Cockson held before 1642 is not certain. The house in Manchester could have been inherited as Henry's portion of the Houghend estate. The lands in Hale and Baguley could have been part of his wife's marriage portion. The property in Chester could have been inherited (most gentry families had a house in Chester), but, on the other hand, it could have been acquired after the Civil War when impoverished Royalists, paying off delinquency fines, were selling off parts of their estates.

In 1635 he married Rebecca, sister of Robert Vawdrey of the Riddings, Timperley, who was an agent for the Court of Wards and Livery in the 1630s. Some time before February 1645 Cockson was Solicitor for Sequestrations in Cheshire and contact man for General Sir William Brereton in London. He was not Brereton's servant, but he kept the general informed of the activities of his Cheshire Parliamentarian opponents in London, especially the Booths of Dunham Massey.

'I cannot express the ignominy it hath brought upon the Ches. soldiers and how they stand branded, not in a private assembly, but amongst the representative body of the kingdom. Doubtless there was some strange design hatching in this and others and it is not impossible but it had an intended influence against 155 [Brereton], whereof, if I mistake not, some of my former letters have given a hint of some such like intentions in brewing.'

In this letter Cockson was warning Brereton that the Booths were trying to influence Parliament against him to take away his commission under the Self-denying Ordinance.[11]

Henry Cockson's influence, though it may have galled him to acknowledge it, helped Robert Tatton survive during the Interregnum. Cockson extended his help to Robert Tatton's brother-in-law and neighbour, Edward Legh, when the widow of Edward's elder brother, Richard, Brigit Harrington, a member of a wealthy and influential Parliamentarian family, claimed the rents of Baguley under the terms of her husband's will. The Deputy Lieutenants of Cheshire supported Brigit Harrington, so Brereton supported Edward Legh, despite the fact that he was a Royalist. Cockson petitioned Parliament in the name of Edward's younger, unmarried sister, Frances. At first the Committee for Compounding briefly granted Baguley to Edward Legh then rescinded the order in favour of Richard's widow. In October 1650 Parliament rescinded the order in favour of Edward Legh, who had by then paid his composition fine.[12]

With William Barrett, the Sequestration agent for Macclesfield and Independent preacher at Ringway and Stockport, and two others, Cockson was appointed sub-commissioner for Cheshire in May 1650.[13] He kept the post and that of Solicitor for Sequestrations in Cheshire until the end of 1659.

Henry Cockson must have felt that he was being pulled in two directions. His position as Solicitor for Sequestrations and Sub-commissioner must have often conflicted with his family loyalties, especially between 1646 and 1652 when his cousin was compounding for his delinquency and trying to pay his fine. But it is largely due to the efforts of Henry Cockson and his brother-in-law Peter Brereton that Robert Tatton still held Wythenshawe Hall in 1660.

Surviving Under Parliamentarian Rule

Although the Tatton family, and Mistress Anne Tatton in particular, during the years 1642-1647 when her husband was from home, were lucky to have Henry Cockson and Anne's Parliamentarian brothers, Thomas and Peter as their guardian angels throughout the period, that did not make life easier when dealing with the Macclesfield Sequestrators and their agents. In fact they probably only mitigated the worst effects in times of emergency. Cockson and Peter Brereton were away in London a great deal of the time.

Reading between the lines of Richard Button's reports to the Sequestrators, Mistress Anne was doing her utmost to foil Parliamentarian attempts to control the Tatton estates and make money out of them, including taking advantage of the opportunity afforded by Prince Rupert's march north which ended in the battle of Marsden Moor.

'by reason of those 2 yeares wch were sor distracted and flyinge before the Army of Prince Rupert, Mrs. Tatton put in a man to looke to the ground & soe till after the fight at Yorke much of the proffitts of the demesne were lost by the meanes of troupers & others wch brought goods & cattell into the ground.'[14]

Robert Tatton probably took advantage of Prince Rupert's march to move to Chester with Edward Legh and his family. Mistress Anne did her best to ensure that her husband and his step-father, Dr Nicholls, received the rents due. She probably used the distraction of Prince Maurice's (younger brother of Rupert) march into Chester in mid-February 1645 when the Parliamentarian army had drawn off from Chester, to travel to the city with the money. She was certainly in Chester by March 10th, 1645, the date of a pass signed by old Sir George Booth. Two other ladies, Mary Dutton and Elizabeth Massey, daughter of Sir William Massey of Puddington (a known recusant family), were to travel with her as far as Dunham, Sir George's home, under the escort of a Tatton servant, William Tomlinson, his man and Mistress Massey's servant.

'To all colonels, Captains, Officers and Soldiers for the King and Parliament'
[10-3-45 Dunham [Massey]] 'For as much as my cousin, Mistress Anne Tatton, wife of Robert Tatton of Whittingshaw [Wythenshawe] Esq., had occasion and liberty to go to Chester to her husband and is now desirous to return to Withingshaw to her little children with whom she desires to live, they for the present being left destitute of help and comfort from father or mother, and because I understand Sir Wm. Brereton had promised not to hinder her return, these are to will and require you to permit this bearer, Wm. Tomlinson, and his man with their horses to pass to Chester for the bringing back of Mistress Tatton to Withinshaw and Mistress Mary, the daughter of Mr. Dutton. And likewise to permit Mistress Elizabeth Massey, daughter of Sir Wm. Massey with her man and horse, to come in their company to Dunham, if she be in readiness when Mistress Tatton sets forward.'[15]

Eight days later Anne Tatton and her party were stopped by a Parliamentarian patrol from Tarvin, half a day's ride (five miles) to the east of Chester. The Parliamentarian garrison commander, Captain William Davies, found amongst Mistress Anne's baggage letters from Royalist ladies in Chester to Royalist ladies in Manchester, members of the Moseley family of Houghend, Withington near Manchester. The content of the letters was the uncertain position of the governor of Chester, Lord John Byron (his post was not confirmed until mid-March) and the advanced pregnancy of his wife, who wanted to go to Wales 'because she thinks Wales is safer than where my sister is'.[16] All information of interest to the Parliamentarians.

Anne Tatton was returned to Chester with her escort. She was unfortunate to have fallen into the hands of a Parliamentarian patrol. She would have had a good chance of delivering the letters safely to the Moseleys. According to a letter sent the same day to Brereton at Middlewich, Tarvin was surrounded by Royalist garrisons and had great difficulty getting messengers through eastwards to Middlewich. When Mistress Anne did return to Wythenshawe Hall is not known, but she had a good opportunity to do so during the chaos caused by Prince Rupert's brief march into Cheshire a day or two after her return to Chester.

Substantial sums of money were spent by Richard Button and others in the repair and upkeep of various parts of the manors of Northenden and Etchells, principally Northenden Mill.

'Payments to ___
    Richard Button of Northenden which hee had laide down for the Reparacion of Northenden Millne and to the saide Richard for the Reparacion of Northenden weare.'[17]

Even so many of the people of Northenden and Etchells seem not to have liked the fact that the Parliamentarians took their rents rather than the lord of the manor. William Barrett noted in his Accounts of Expenditure for Northenden Parish in 1644 -

'Item spent uppon Souldiers that went wth mee   0 3 0
(Edmund Shelmerdyne) to destrayne for the Rents'[18]

The sequestrators also collected and then disbursed the leys (local rates) to the local constables. Normally the constables (there were two each for Northenden and Etchells) would collect the leys with the help of assessors appointed by the Court Leets. William Barrett's accounts show two disbursements of money to the Constables of Etchells between July 1645 and the end of May, 1645.

'Item To the Constables of Etchells for leyes for
Peele, Withinshawe and Whiteleggs house   00 19 06

Item To the Constables of Etchells for leyes for
Peele Sept.12, 1646, for quartering of soldiers   00 19 00
and for Warrington Bridge [the repair of][19]

The sequestrators did meet at least once in Northenden (April 4th, 1644) and in Etchells at Gatley (July 23rd, 1644) for which they claimed 10s and 4s 2d respectively.[20] (Was the dinner so much more sumptuous at the Boat than at the Gatley hostelry.)

William Barrett, despite the fact that he was an Independent preacher, did spend some money on the refurbishment of Northenden Church, especially in repairing the chancel floor and the chancel windows which were damaged by Colonel Duckenfield's troops during the siege of Wythenshawe Hall.[21]

The Macclesfield Sequestrators gave a part of the glebe lands to Captain Edmund Shelmerdine. Parts of the demesne land of Peele was also leased to Francis Shelmerdine, Reginald Kelsall (of Bradshawe Hall, Cheadle) and Captain Richard Grantham. This was probably partly to oversee the activities of Thomas Mallory and Dr Nicholls, farming and otherwise.[22]

The Macclesfield Sequestrators were obliged to pay a fifth of the value of the property to the wives of delinquents for the maintenance of themselves and their children. Mistress Anne Tatton and Mistress Mary Mallory, both with five or six children each, were paid a fifth part regularly. But a fifth of what? In good years the manors of Northenden and Etchells (excluding that part which formed Mrs Nicholls' dowry) could provide nearly £309 a year.[23] But I doubt very much if half of that could have been raised by the tenants (small though the rents were) between 1643 and 1649. The years of war and disruption were followed by years of bad harvest. So it is quite likely that Mistress Tatton, her six children, indoor and outdoor servants, were not given more than £40 to £50 a year on which to live, and probably a great deal less.

Not only did the Tatton family and the Tatton tenants have to suffer the pryings and impositions of the sequestration agents, they also had to suffer the privations of passing armies. In May 1644 Prince Rupert, on his famous march north which ended at Marston Moor, probably passed through Northenden and Etchells on his way to cross the Mersey at Stockport. He took horses and other provisions from William Davenport of Bramhall and was probably given what provisions could be spared by Mistress Anne Tatton.

The Parliamentarian General Sir William Brereton drew off most of his troops (Scots, Lancashire and Yorkshire men as well as Cheshire men) from around Chester and billeted them both sides of the Mersey around Stockport in the spring of 1645, thinking that Rupert might try that same route again. In May 1645 the Scots Army, billeted in Northenden and Etchells, paid for their provisions with Scottish tuppenny pieces, which were either counterfeit or not considered proper payment. Almost in the same month Sir William Brereton's dragooners ate three measures of oats. Those who suffered from the counterfeit pennies and the oats eaten by the Scots Army and Brereton's troops were compensated by the local constables but this was probably only the tip of the iceberg, payments that had to be made because of hardship. Because there was not the money to pay compensation to all, troops were virtually free quartered.[24]

The quartering and provisioning of the Yorkshire horse in April and May 1645 (just before the harvesting of summer fruits and vegetables, when food was often short, even in good years) was a great burden to the people around Stockport, including Etchells. A petition was sent from 'the oppressed inhabitants and soldiers within the parishes of Stockport and Prestbury in the Hundred of Macclesfield to Sir William Brereton' before 9th May, 1645 stating that:

'Many of your petitioners, by reason of the many taxations, leys and impositions which, by the occasion o9f the troubles of these times, have been and still are are upon us (besides the charge and maintenance of the trained and freehold bands), are not able to subsist, especially at this present. The maintaining of the garrison at Hoole, the provisions thither weekly sent and the burden of quartering Yorks. horse lies heavy upon them, so as they neither can nor will endure it.'[25]

The petitioners asked that the Yorkshire horse be moved away, otherwise they would not levy leys or maintain the soldiers at Hoole.

A letter from Colonel Robert Duckenfield to Brereton dated May 12th, 1645 confirmed what the petitioners said. His men, manning the garrison at Hoole, were anxious about the safety and wellbeing of their families in and around Stockport. Some of Duckenfield's men, under Captain Edmund Shelmerdine and Captain Alcock, came from Northenden and Etchells.

'I received notice just now that the Yorks regt under Lt. Col. Spencer is quartered about Stockport and in Mottram parish and intend to tender the ruin of these parts, as well as about Macclesfield. They take very many horses and much money and goods and neglect your orders. I desire you will consider so far of our neighbours' miseries as to be assured my regt will be gone home within these three days only [i.e. unless] they have certain notice that the horse aforesaid be removed out of their quarters.'

A petition by Duckenfield's regiment was sent on the same day, asking that the Yorkshire horse be moved.

'...having for three weeks past...been burdened with such as pretend themselves to be friends and yet lie devouring and depriving them of their estates at home, not being content with such provisions of victuals as they have to relieve their poor families withal, but daily threatening them if they provide not better, protesting also that they will not removed their quarters until they have either eaten them up or beaten out of them. In the meantime wounding and abusing such of our friends and neighbours as do not observe their commands.'[26]

Brereton sent some of the arrears of payment to the Yorkshire horse and they moved south from Stockport to Adlington two days later. But by May 23rd, 1645 Brereton was camped on Barlow Moor with his own horse and the Staffordshire horse and dragoons quartered nearby, partly in Northenden.[27] Sir William planned a rendezvous on Barlow Moor for Stafford, Lancashire, Cheshire and Lord Fairfax's horse, from where he would block most of the fords and bridges into Lancashire against the King and his army. In the event the King did not march further into Cheshire than Market Drayton before turning south again.

In economic terms, the consequences of the Civil War, the movement of and quartering of troops round and about, would have been terrible for the people of Northenden and Etchells. There are no figures for the two manors, but there are for other places in Cheshire. Lymm, a village on the main Warrington road, suffered a cost of £1,164 in taxes, free quarter to troops and plundered goods. Parliamentarian forces also took fifty-one horses from Lymm. In other places cattle, often the chief economic source for many people in Cheshire, were driven off. In January 1646 the deputy lieutenant of Cheshire ruled that the level of taxation was too high in some sequestered township, so they were given a rebate of 25% back-dated for two years. This was to reduce the risk of people being tempted to join the Royalists.

The years of disrupted agriculture resulted in widespread famine throughout England. Northenden and Etchells did not escape. The disruption and the famine resulted in two things, an increase in the number of people on the Poor Rate and a large jump in corn prices.

In good years Northenden and Etchells probably grew enough corn (wheat, oats, barley and rye) for home consumption and a little more to sell at Stockport or Manchester markets. But in the years following the Civil War grains prices soared. In Cheshire the JPs brought the prices down swiftly, but even so one Tatton tenant, John Ryle of High Greaves in Etchells, noted very high prices at Stockport on April 6th, 1649.

'Oats at foure pounds the bushell
Wheate at   2li. 13. 4
Beans at   2li. 8. 0
Barley at 2li the bushell or upward'[28]

Notes

1. J Ry L Tatton Family Papers, document no. 341.
2. Earwaker Vol 1.
3. A.G. Matthews, editor, *Calamy Revised*.
4. Earwaker, Vol 1, p.293 (B.L. Harleian mss 2130, f.134 and f.209).
5. J Ry L Tatton Family Papers, doc. no. 341, a list of freeholders dated 1666; the 1648 Rental Survey (a nineteenth century copy) mentions an Edward Shelmerdine as owning the freehold 14 acres. This could either be the father of Edmund Shelmerdine or a mistake by the copyist.
6. Quoted in Earwaker.
7. R.N. Dore, editor, *The Letter Books of Sir William Brereton*, Vol I (Vol 123), item no 385.
8. The last two names and Thomas Massey are from a list of pensioners at Stockport dated 1653, quoted in Earwaker, Vol 2., p.68-9.
9. William Davenport of Bramhall's Commonplace and Memorandum Book, quoted in Ormerod, Vol 9 (Morten facsimile edition), p.826.
10. J Ry L Tatton Family Papers, doc. 195, 1648 Rental Survey.
11. *The Letter Books of Sir William Brereton*, Vol I (Vol 123), items nos. 20, 350, and 364.
12. Ibid, item no. 389 and the editor's notes; Calendar of the Proceedings of the Committee for Compounding (CPCC).
13. (CPCC).
14. B.L. Harleian ms. 2126, ff. 131.
15. *The Letter Books of Sir William Brereton*, Vol I (Vol 123), item no. 27.
16. Ibid, items nos. 71, 72, 73, 74.
17. B.L. Harleian ms. 2126, ff. 131.
18. B.L. Harleian ms. 2130, ff. 209.
19. Ibid.
20. Ibid.
21. Ibid.
22. Ibid.
23. J Ry L Tatton Family Papers, 1648 Rental Survey.
24. B.L. Harleian ms. 2130 f.209. From the accounts of moneys disbursed it seems that William Barrett might have been paying out more money than he raised from Northenden and Etchells; *Cheshire 1630-1660*, p.107.
25. *The Letter Books of Sir William Brereton*, Vol I, item no.452.
26. Ibid, items 499 and 501.
27. Ibid, items 607 and 621.
28. John Ryle's Memorandum Book, facsimile by Frank Mitchell, copy in Stockport Library.

5

The End of Fighting

Robert Tatton in Chester and Oxford, March 1644 – June 1646

According to a warrant of Lord Byron, giving the amount of food in each household in Chester towards the end of the 'Leaguer' or siege, Robert Tatton was living in St Martin's Ward, probably on or near Whitefriars. He had with him, according to the warrant, seven servants and two soldiers (probably Robert Renshawe and William Smith).[1]

Edward Legh and his family were living in St Michael's Ward, although his son Henry was baptised in St Oswald's Church, the parish church in Northgate sited in the Cathedral Close, on August 12th, 1644.[2] The Leghs were probably living on Bridge Street or Pepper Street, not far from Robert Tatton.

After the death of Dean Thomas Mallory on April 3rd, 1644, Dr Nicholls was very quickly appointed to the vacant post and so moved into the Deanery in the grounds of the Cathedral. In a receipt attached to a rental of his wife's tenants William Nicholls styled himself 'Doctor of Divinity & Deane of the Cathedral Church of Christ & the Virgin Mary in Chester'.[3]

In a city under siege disease, as well as hunger, was rife. Five months after Henry's birth little Anne Legh died and was buried in the Church of St Mary-on-the-Hill, near the Castle, at the southern end of the city.

> 'Anne, daughter of Mr. Leigh of Baguley, esqr. buried in the Chancell 29th day December [1644]'.[4]

If Robert Tatton had financial problems before the Civil War they were as nothing compared to the ones he was facing now (and those he would face after the First Civil War), keeping a very small household in Chester on the rents that Anne brought in March 1644.

Sometime before January 1644/45 Tatton and Nicholls borrowed £32 from a Chester alderman, Christopher Blease, a wealthy mercer. Later, between January 1644/45 and March 1644/45 they entered into a bond with Lord Cholmondley to borrow £109 1s 8d. The modern day equivalent is over £20,000. Probably, though the bond does not mention it, Wythenshawe Hall, the demesne lands, Peel Hall and its demesne lands were used as surety.[5]

In November 1644 Brereton began the 'Leaguer' of Chester with Cheshire and Staffordshire troops as well as Irish troops who had changed sides after the battle of Nantwich. He had scanty forces and the difficulties were enormous. Most of the fervent Royalists in Cheshire were concentrated in the city, together with a large garrison of 3,000 men, and formidable defences. He established a forward base at Tarvin and positioned forces in an inner and outer ring. The outer ring comprised detachments outside the Royalist Beeston Castle and Farndon on the River Dee to 'to prevent raiding on the backs of the besiegers' and the inner ring was made up of garrisons at Oulton Hall, Huxley Hall, Tattenhall, Aldford,

Barrow and Christleton, the latter less than a mile from the city. Lord John Byron, governor of Chester, attacked all these positions with some success. The Beeston besiegers were wiped out while at dinner. Christleton was attacked but Byron's troops were ambushed and driven back into the city with losses.

Byron appealed to Oxford for help and the King sent Prince Maurice. But the Prince's own force was so weak he had to augment them from other garrisons on the way up, thus losing the Royalist stronghold of Shrewsbury to the ever vigilant Colonel Mytton. Prince Rupert quickly marched up from Hereford to aid his brother and forced Brereton to abandon the siege of Chester and Beeston in February 1645.[6] The latter soon realised that 'the Princes have left Chester in a worse condition than they found it'.[7] They took Byron's best Irish troops and left him with only the town guard and a Welsh regiment.

Brereton returned to the 'Leaguer' in March 1645 with Yorkshire, Staffordshire and Lancashire troops and an elaborate network of positions, to break the link with Wales, as well as the old ones on the eastern side. At the beginning of May Brereton reported that all three sieges were going well. But by the end of the month the King and Prince Maurice were marching up through the Midlands to rescue Chester. Brereton was reluctant to pull back from the sieges until the King reached Market Drayton, just six miles from the Cheshire border. Then only did he withdraw beyond the Mersey. But, instead of moving north to Chester, as Brereton and his officers expected, the King swerved east from Market Drayton towards Leicester and defeat at the hands of the New Model Army at Naseby.[8]

The 'Leaguer' was resumed under the joint command of Jones, Lothian, and the County Committee, while Brereton rode south to Westminster to see Parliament renew his exemption from the Self-Denying Ordinance, as it had done for Oliver Cromwell. Little was done about the 'Leaguer' until September when the unwelcome rumour of Brereton's reappointment to his command reached the ears of the County Committee (no doubt Cockson and other friends had kept Brereton informed of the lack of progress, especially since the County Committee was dominated by the Booths and their adherents). On September 19th, the besiegers made an assault on the north-west suburbs with 500 horse, 200 dragoons and 700 foot, but with little success.

Then the news came that the King was at Chirk, a mere day's march away, and the whereabouts of his Parliamentarian shadow, General Poyntz, unknown. The King, with his Life Guards and Lord Gerard's troop of horse, entered the city on September 23rd, whilst the main body of cavalry, under Sir Marmaduke Langdale, crossed the river at Holt and camped on Miller's Heath, three miles south-east of the city. Jones and Lothian sent off a messenger to find General Poyntz. The man was captured on his return, so the Royalists knew that

Poyntz was marching up from Whitchurch to the aid of Jones and Lothian, though the latter did not.

The battle of Rowton Heath took place on September 24th, in which the 'leaguer' troops, aided towards the end by General Poyntz, roundly defeated the King's Lifeguards and the Chester garrison.

By dusk the Royalists, or at last those still alive, had fled, some into Wales across the Holt Bridge, some further into Cheshire, and a few, the garrison and town guard presumably, tried to struggle back into Chester through the Northgate, Robert Tatton, Edward Legh and Dr Nicholls amongst them.[9] Over 1,000 Royalists died in the battle, including a cousin of the King, the young Earl of Lichfield. The King watched the disaster from the Phoenix Tower, then moved to St Werburgh's Tower.

'The sad disaster of this day the king (good man) beholds from the Phoenix tower, from whence he moved to St. Werburgh's steeple, where as he was talking with a captaine, a bullet from St. John's gave him a salute, narrowly missing the king, hit the said Captaine in the head, who died in his place.'[10]

Charles left the next day, all hopes of joining with Montrose dashed, and marched south into Wales with the remnant of his Life Guards. The final phase of the 'Leaguer' began, a slow starvation with intermittant bombardment. Towards the end of the siege hungry people pursued Lord Byron through the streets with threats and pleadings. Where there had been high morale there was now just a struggle to live from day-to-day. Brereton blocked all Chester's supply lines. The sheriff of Chester was shot dead whilst on watch. Gradually hope of relief from either the King or from Sir William Vaughan in Wales receded. Byron began to negotiate and 12 commissioners were appointed on each side to decide on the surrender tèrms.

After Michaelmas 1645 Robert Tatton began to play an important part in the final phase of the 'Leaguer' when he was elected High Sheriff of Cheshire. He was only truly Sheriff for the four months until the surrender of Chester. The Parliamentarians then elected Henry Brooke of Norton Priory Sheriff for the remainder of his year of office, although Robert was probably still considered the true Sheriff whilst he was in Oxford. Most of the documents that survive from those few short months show him acting, together with Charles Walley, Mayor of Chester from 1644 to 1646, as an intermediary in the negotiations for the surrender of Chester.

Walley was the 'principal means of the surrender of the city'.[11] He had been one of the city leaders in almost constant conflict with the various governors, Legge, Shipman, Sir Nicholas Byron and his nephew, Lord John Byron, over the firing of the Handbridge suburb, and various other points. Walley was also one of those who favoured the concentration of Royalist resources in Cheshire on the city, the policy which had isolated Robert Tatton at Wythenshawe Hall.

Tatton and Walley, with others, prevailed on Byron to sue for peace and from January 15th onwards became go-betweens, chivvying the governor, trying to keep the negotiations going for the sake of Chester and its people.

'At the entreaty of us, the mayor, noblemen and gents., aldermen and citizens of Chester, Lord Byron, our governor, in whom the whole power of treaty rests, is pleased to give way to a treaty upon honourable conditions. To which, if you assent, commissioners to that purpose may be agreed upon by both sides.'

Colonel Robert Duckenfield and Major James Lothian replied for Brereton two days later

'Notwithstanding that your former rejections of fair and honourable conditions and the expense of time and blood (which hath been occasioned by your obstinacy) might justly provoke him to refuse any further treaty, yet that it may appear that he retains his wonted desires of the preservation of the city and the lives and estates of the inhabitants, if your governor (in whom you say lies the full power to treat) sends out reasonable propositions betwixt this and Monday noon, he will take them into consideration and return such answer as may stand with honour and justice and may prevent the destruction of this ancient city.'

Lord Byron replied with a list of twelve commissioners on January 19th but asked for more time to compose his propositions. Brereton gave him a further day. After that the negotiations got underway, but not without hitches.

'My Lord Byron has acquainted us with a letter which he received from you the last night...by which we conceive you apprehend a rejection of your proposition, which we must wonder at, well knowing that my Lord writ unto you to appoint an indifferent place, where our and your commissioners might meet, to treat upon the propositions implying so much, and you having so often by letter expressed your tender care of the city's preservation, and prevention of the effusion of blood. Our desire therefore is that you will nominate your commissioners, with the time and place, that ours and yours may meet to debate and treat upon the propositions tendered on both sides, without there can be no hopes of a conclusion.'

Brereton replied the same day, January 29th.

'Gentlemen, your several dilatory answers I have received and do assure that if the Lord Byron in whom (you say) the sole power to treate resteth, do not consent and act therein, you may forbear sending. Do not deceive yourselves in expectation that I will treat when you please. I am sorry my care for the city's preservation hath produced such unsuitable effects. The further misery that is like to befall the city be on your heads...'[12]

The last attempt at relief was scattered by Colonel Mytton on January 24th. After that Lord Byron took the negotiations more seriously. The twelve Chester Commissioners met with Brereton's Commissioners on January 30th. The following day, despite the Chester Commissioners' wish to postpone further negotiations until Monday next – perhaps in the vain hope that more relief was on its way, the conditions of surrender were concluded.[13] Lord Byron, his officers, their wives and families, and a few soldiers, marched out of Chester to Conway on February 2nd. The Welsh soldiers and citizens of Chester were to remained unmolested, the former to return to their homes, the latter to go about their own business. But all cannon, arms, powder, shot and horses (those not deemed to be needed by Lord Byron's small group of soldiers) were to be collected together and handed over to Brereton. Those soldiers of Irish parentage were to stay in the city as prisoners.[14]

At the end of the siege Robert Tatton and some of his servants made their way to the Royalist headquarters at Oxford after the surrender of Chester with Lord Byron's force. Dr Nicholls rode out of Chester, first to Conway, then on to Denbigh (which surrendered on October 26th).[15] Edward Legh escorted his wife, his mother-in-law and his four young children home to Baguley Hall, clutching a safe conduct pass signed by Sir William Brereton. Two days after the surrender of Chester he began compounding for his delinquency as a Royalist, claiming that he had gone to Chester in the first place to call in some debts. (which needed to be witnessed by his wife and children?)[16]

By March Oxford was under siege from the New Model Army, commanded by Commissary General Henry Ireton, Cromwell's son-in-law. On April 29th the King slipped out of Oxford. A week later he surrendered to the Scots at Newark and the First Civil War was nearly at an end. Six weeks after that Oxford surrendered to Sir Thomas Fairfax, Commander-in-Chief of the New Model Army.

Robert Tatton and his servants, like the rest of the garrison, were allowed to leave Oxford for London, with a printed safe-conduct pass in Tatton's pocket signed by Fairfax.[17]

On June 24th, 1646, Robert Tatton surrendered to Parliamentarian forces for the third and final time. He had fought for his home and his king for nearly four years. Oxford was the last time he took up arms.

Compounding for delinquency and financial problems for the Tatton family, July 1646 – April 1657

As soon as the siege of Oxford ended Robert Tatton began compounding for delinquency in order to save his estates and hall from the sequestrators. Amongst the Tatton Family Papers in John Rylands Library, Manchester there are three safe-conduct passes, two hand-written, one printed, issued to Robert Tatton between July 1646 and March 1647, giving information on his movements in that period.[18] Robert rode straight from Oxford to London, to Goldsmith's Hall, to apply to the Committee for Confiscations. On July 3rd he returned to Wythenshawe but by December he was back in London. The printed safe-conduct pass allowed Tatton to stay in the city for an unspecified length of time until he had 'perfected' his compounding for delinquency. It was issued on an order from the House of Commons. There were so many Royalists in London at this time that these safe-conduct passes were used as licences to sort out those authorised to be in the city from those no who might be plotting the overthrow of Parliament.

Robert was very unlucky with his compounding. Had the border of Bucklow Hundred been two miles further east (in its Domesday Book position) he would have been under the jurisdiction of the moderate Booth-controlled sequestration committee, like his brothers-in-law, Edward Legh and Richard Brereton, and his uncle by marriage, James Massey of Sale. Instead throughout much of 1646 and 1647 Anne Tatton was faced, as she

had been for the past two years, with the most severe and zealous of all the hundredal committees, the Macclesfield Sequestrators. The latter comprised three members, Colonel Henry Bradshawe of Marple (brother of the Lord President of the High Court which tried Charles I for treason in January, 1649), Colonel Robert Duckenfield, whose men took Wythenshawe Hall for Parliament, and John Legh of Knutsford Booths.

The Macclesfield Sequestrators, in direct contravention of an order of the House of Commons, threatened Anne Tatton with the sale of the demesne of Wythenshawe Hall, the mills and the twin manors (they had already sold the cattle to pay off arrears of assessments which should have been paid out of the tenants' rents). In desperation, Anne wrote to the Committee for Confiscations at Goldsmith's Hall some time between November 1646 and March 1647 (when Robert was away in London compounding).

She also suggested that:

'the Sequestrators in Cheshire to lett her or her friends (whom she will nominate) have the said demeanes lands rents and mills for this yeare insueing giveing as much as any other will give and securing the same, as above to Command the Tenants to pay the Charges and assessm[en]t to the use of the State out of the rents remayninge in theire hands by yor hon[oura]ble Order so aforesaid.'[19]

Robert Tatton was fined £806 10s (a tenth of the value of his estate) by the Macclesfield Committee, which was confirmed by the Committee for Compounding on December 5th, 1646. He appealed on December 22nd and begged for a review on account of the overvaluing of the customary rents and asked for the allowance of a rent-charge of £13 a year on the demesne lands, about which he had previously omitted to tell the Committee. He also asked to be allowed to pay his fine by installments and not in one lump sum, which he could not afford. On August 28th, 1646 the Committee for Compounding noted that Robert had neglected payment of his fine. Six months later, on March 3rd, 1649 the fine was reduced to £707 13s 4d and a month later, after paying it, on April 11th, he was allowed to 'enjoy his estate'.[20]

But the Macclesfield Sequestrators were determined to control the Tatton estates as much as they could. By 1646 they had already put their own tenants into the manors of Wythenshawe and Etchells. By July 1645 some of the parsonage lands of Thomas Mallory were already in the hands of Captain Edmund Shelmerdine, although 'Mrs. Mallory the delinquents wyfe holds the said p'sonage house'.[21] 'Mr. Francis Shelmerdine, Mr. Reginald Kelsall and Captain Richard Grantham' of Cheadle also tenanted land from the Wythenshawe estates leased to them by the Committee.[22] Two of the above were outsiders but good Parliamentarians. Reginald Kelsall of Bradshawe Hall, Cheadle had 28 Cheshire acres in Etchells, a large amount of land amongst the small tenants of the manor.[23]

Whilst Anne was writing to Goldsmith Hall, Robert recruited the support of Sir Thomas Fairfax in his fight against the Macclesfield Sequestrators. Fairfax had the reputation of being a courteous and fair-minded man. Robert wanted him to verify to the Sequestration Committee that he was entitled to benefit of the Articles of Oxford, which they seemed to doubt, and that it was because the Quarter Sessions had not taken place in Chester due to plague that he had not paid his fine (transactions such as the sale of land and the writing of new title deeds had to be done at the Quarter Sessions). Fairfax obliged and wrote to the Macclesfield Sequestrators, even though he was in the midst of the Putney Debates, the great debate of the New Model Army at Putney to determine whether ordinary men should be given the vote or not.[24]

The effect of this letter was to lessen the harassment from Macclesfield Sequestrators. The suggestion of leasing the demesne lands to friends was taken up. This was a concession given to only a few in dire straits and possibly the additional influence of Henry Cockson and Anne's brother, Peter, with all their contacts in London had helped.[25] Robert Tatton nominated his three brothers-in-law, Richard Brereton, Alexander Barlowe (now on the Parliamentarian Committee for Manchester), Edward Legh, his uncle James Massey, who was compounding for delinquency himself, Robert Brereton of Middlesex (perhaps a cousin of Anne's) and Peter Legh of Lyme, Edward Legh's cousin. The terms under which the lands were to be leased were set out in an indenture. A draft of this deed survives amongst the Tatton Family Papers, undated, with a note in the margin signed by one Ralph Worthington (perhaps the brother of Roger Worthington of Cross Acres) and dated March 24th, 1647/48.[26]

As well as his own troubles, Robert Tatton was financially supporting his mother and step-father. Dr Nicholls was ill-treated by Parliamentarian soldiers and imprisoned following the surrender of Denbigh Castle in October 1646, which was contrary to the Articles of Surrender for Denbigh. In March 1647 his fine was assessed at £143, mostly on his wife's property, the demesne lands of Peel Hall and the Etchells rents of Heathhouses, Bolshawe, Woodhouse Lane, Shadow Moss, Cross Acres and Poundswick.[27]

Two tenants who were part of the garrison of Wythenshawe, William Smith and Robert Renshawe, also compounded for delinquency. William Smith had been taken prisoner after the surrender of the hall and was assessed at £1. Robert Renshawe, who had gone to Chester and Oxford with his lord, was assessed at £3 10s.

Robert Tatton had creditors pressing on all sides, the Macclesfield Sequestrators amongst them of course. He owed his brothers-in-law, Thomas Brereton and Richard Brereton (who was also compounding for his delinquency), £1,244 and £420 respectively. Thomas Gerard was owed £420 and there was also the £109 (now £209 because of a penalty clause in the counterbond) borrowed from Lord Cholmondley in Chester, who desperately needed the money to pay his own very heavy delinquency fine. Altogether Robert Tatton owed £3,000. This was not a large amount for a member of the county gentry to owe to friends and relatives in the seventeenth

century, but the privations and fines resultant on the Civil War had caused his creditors to call in debts.[28] Added to this, Robert had not been able to collect the rents and dues from his tenants for the two years to the end of 1648.

Robert needed desperately to raise money. He offered all his Wythenshawe estates as security on a mortgage of £2,500. Sometime in October 1647, through the cleric Ralph Brideoak, who was then in the service of the Earl of Derby, Tatton applied to a wealthy, retired Manchester clothier, Humphrey Chetham, for a loan. Chetham replied on October 24th.

'If you will convey unto mee your whole estate not onely in Wythenshawe and Northen, and the milles, but also in Peele and Etchells, its like I shall furnish you with 1250li [£1,250] for the present to take of your sequestration and the statute, and make you a lease of all back again – 100li [£100] per ann[u]m'.[29]

The money was not enough and Chetham wanted Mrs Nicholls's dower lands included. But Robert desperately needed the full £2,500. A year later he wrote to John Rogerson, a Manchester lawyer, and through him, offered Chetham first refusal on the mortgage of Wythenshawe Hall and Northenden October 28th, 1648.

'I received a letter this day from Mr. Tatton...Theere is an extent now to be sitten against his land att the suite of Major Radcliffe, the unnecessary charge whereof hee would faine avoid (if it was possible), and therefore is resolved to sell the mannours of Withenshawe and Northen, and therefore desire you have the first refusall of an absolute sale thereof, for the Halle of Withinshawe is known to be as gallant a seate as any Cheshire affords.'[30]

A few days later, through Ralph Brideoak again, Robert offered his mother's dower lands as additional security. Chetham now agreed to lend the full amount. On November 8th, Ralph Brideoak wrote to Humphrey Chetham on Robert's behalf, clinching the deal. Only just in time according to Brideoak's letter.

'Sr, I shall not need to importune you againe in this behalfe, having found you so much inclined of yor owne accord to doe him what courtesy you may; only I humbly crave leave to remember you [tha]t dispatch in this business does much exalt yor favour; his children, his creditors, his estate, and honour called for a speedy hand to deliver them from absolute ruin.'[31]

A draft of the covenant dated December 29th, 1648 stated that Chetham would lend Tatton the £2,500 to be paid back at £260 per year. The covenant itself, written in Latin on parchment, was dated January 5th, 1648/49. Robert made a rental survey of the tenancies of the manor of Northenden and Etchells, the rents and services due, together with the fields of the demesne lands of Wythenshawe and Peele, for Humphrey Chetham.[32] In October 1649 Robert Tatton borrowed a further £500, bringing the total capital sum borrowed to £3,000.[33]

This large loan to Robert may be the reason why Humphrey Chetham suddenly dropped negotiations to buy the sixteenth century college buildings in Manchester from the Earl of Derby. Chetham must have thought Tatton's need greater than the fulfilment of an old man's dream. Chetham's Hospital, with places for twelve poor boys, was established by the latter's will and the interest and repayment of the £3,000 loan paid for it. Alexander Barlowe, Anne Tatton's brother-in-law, was one of the first feoffees, or governors, of the hospital.

But Robert's financial problems did not end there. In 1650 he wrote to Colonel Henry Bradshawe to appeal against the amount he was being charged for the raising of soldiers to fight Charles Stuart and the Scots at Preston and Worcester. He thought his condition should be considered. Bradshawe replied on October 4th that 'if it appeared that he was injured, there was no doubt, but on signifying so much to them, he would be redressed'.[34] Robert was assessed and fined £500. He claimed that he had compounded on the Oxford Articles and requested a discharge from assessment. The Committee for the Advancement of Money disagreed. They pointed out that the Oxford Articles had a time limit of six months and Robert had taken over two and a half years to perfect his composition. But Robert had not been tardy. He had spent a great deal of time travelling to London to perfect his composition. But Fairfax and his officers had been over-optimistic in the speed taken to compound and for impoverished Royalists to pay fines. Tatton was re-assessed at £260 with a promise to be heard as to his debts when he had paid half of the fine. A year later he was discharged under the Act of Pardon.[35]

In 1656 Robert Tatton was again forced to consider selling or remortgaging Northenden and Etchells. George Chetham, Humphrey's nephew and heir, was buying the collegiate buildings in Manchester from the Earl of Derby's heirs and setting up Chetham's Hospital under the terms of his uncle's will. Therefore he was demanding payment of the rest of the mortgage from Robert. At the same time Robert was in arrears with the payment of interest on a loan from a gentleman named John Bennett and he was probably also being pressed for payment of the Decimation Tax on ex-Royalists. In a letter dated February 3rd, 1656/57 Robert offered to raise the money through releasing those tenants with less than three lives left in lease and charging them with a heavy entrance fine into new leases (a very common way for landed gentry to raise money in the seventeenth century). On the same day, Robert wrote to someone he called 'Cozen', asking that he 'treate with mr. Bennett'. Both letters were delivered by Henry Cockson, acting in his capacity as manor steward, but also using his contacts as Solicitor General for Sequestrations for Cheshire.[36]

Negotiations had opened on a mortgage loan of £2,500 in the previous December with two gentlemen, Simon Bennett of Bearhampton, Buckinghamshire and Thomas Russell of St Martin, Ludgate, London. A rough copy of the mortgage agreement was made before Oliver St John, Lord Chief Justice. But Robert had an urgent need for more money to pay off debts and fines. A flurry of letters followed in February and March between Robert and his various agents in London. On March 4th, a fair copy was made of the mortgage agreement between Bennett, Russell and Robert and his debtors.[37]

Perhaps John Bennett was not amenable to the idea, but whatever happened eleven days later Basil Hearne, kinsman to Robert's brother-in-law, Peter Brereton, wrote that someone was interested in lending money on a mortgage bond with the manor of Northenden as security and asked for a schedule of the demesne lands and the tenants' holdings, which is dated March 3rd, 1657.[38] This someone had £28,000 to spend on greater lands than Robert was offering and Peter Brereton questioned whether or not the tenants' lands were over-valued.

'I can say nothing to your values by the acre, onely I wish & hope you have delt so ungeniously in that poyent, as they will upon vieiwe, hold their values.'

He wished that

'with all my hart you had a good free Chapman [a reference to Humphrey Chetham] but such are hard to be gott.'[39]

Robert replied, through Henry Cockson, that he thought the values he had put upon his tenants' holdings were reasonable but for the sake of a quick agreement he would consider lowering them and putting up the manor of Etchells as security as well.[40]

Whether the gentleman did actually put up the money for a mortgage of both manors is not known. The fact that there was no sale of Tatton lands, which might have resulted otherwise, seems to indicate that a mortgage was agreed with someone. If a schedule was made for Etchells, as Henry Cockson said it would be after the next Assizes, then it has since been lost.

The consequences of heavy debts and mortgages resulting mostly from the Civil War period stayed with the Tatton family until the end of the seventeenth century. It wasn't until the mid-eighteenth century that the Tatton family began acquiring land again.

Notes
1. Warrant of Lord Byron, printed in J. Morris, *Siege of Chester*, JCNWAS 1923, Appendix II, p.239. There is mistake – Robert Tatton is referred to as 'Sheriffe Tattnall'.
2. St. Oswald's parish register, printed in *Siege of Chester*, Appendix III, p.245.
3. J Ry L Tatton Family Papers, Rental of Dr Nicholls dated 1643/44 and endorsed on the back with a receipt dated 7th March, 1644/45.
4. St Mary-on-the-Hill Parish Register from Earwaker's 'History of St Mary-on-the-Hill', reprinted in *Siege of Chester*, Appendix III, p.247.
5. J Ry L Tatton Family Papers, Document no.222, bond and counter-bond between Tatton, Nicholls and Lord Cholmondley. The debt was fully repaid in 1649.
6. *Civil Wars in Cheshire*, p.45.
7. Ibid, p.47.
8. Dore, p.49.
9. Dore, p.52.
10. *Siege of Chester*, Appendix I, p.223.
11. *Civil Wars in Cheshire*, p.53.
12. Two letters from *The Letter Books of Sir William Brereton*, Vol. II (Vol.128), items no.1251 and 1255, and two letters reprinted in *Siege of Chester*.
13. *Cheshire Civil War Tracts*, letter from Sir William Brereton to the House of Commons, dated February 2nd, 1645/46, pp.128-29.
14. The Articles of the Surrender of Chester and the list of the 24 Commissioners are in *Cheshire Civil War Tracts*, pp.129-134.
15. A.G. Matthews, editor, *Walker revised: Being a revision of John Walker's 'The Sufferings of the Clergy during the Grand Rebellion, 1642-60'*, p.92.
16. The Calendar of the Committee for Compounding, p.1090.
17. J Ry L Tatton Family Papers, no.285, printed safe-conduct pass.

18. J Ry L Tatton Family Papers, hand-written safe-conducts, London to Wythenshawe, dated July 3rd, 1646, March 19th, 1646/47, printed safe-conduct issued by Goldsmiths Hall under an order from the Houses of Parliament dated December 15th, 1646, no.286.

19. Ibid, document no.287 – a nineteenth century copy of a letter in the Public Record Office.

20. Calendar of the Proceedings of the Committee for Compounding, edited by M A Green, 3 vols, published 1889-92 (CPCC).

21. BL Harleian ms 2130, quoted in Earwaker, vol 1, p.293, accounts for the glebe lands of St Wilfrids, Northenden.

22. BL Harleian ms 2130, f134 and f209, Accounts for Expenditure for Northenden Parish from the Macclesfield Sequestration Committee, quoted in Earwaker, vol 1.

23. Ibid, Account of land let to farm.

24. J Ry L Tatton Family Papers, Letter from Sir Thomas Fairfax to the Committee for Sequestration.

25. *Cheshire, 1630-1660*, Morrill, p.112.

26. *The Letters Books of Sir William Brereton*, item no.389.

27. *Sufferings of the Clergy*; CPCC.

28. Assessment for the delinquency fine (Earwaker); J Ry L Tatton Family Papers, document no.22, bond and counterbond.

29. Letter quoted in *The Life of Humphrey Chetham* by E.R. Raines and C.V. Sutton, Chet. Soc., NS Vol 49, Part 1, p.118.

30. Ibid, p.111; Major Radcliffe was Richard Radcliffe, a Parliamentarian officer from Manchester.

31. Ibid, p.112.

32. J Ry L Tatton Family Papers, document nos.197 (the covenant) and 195 (the 1648 Rental Survey).

33. *The Life of Humphrey Chetham*, Chet. Soc., NS vol 50, Chetham's will, dated 1653.

34. *History of Cheshire*, Vol III, the township of Marple, footnotes.

35. The Calendar of the Committee for the Advancement of Money, Part 3, p.1307.

36. J Ry L Tatton Family Papers no.269 – two letters in rough draft.

37. Ibid, no.1106.

38. Ibid, nos.227, 347.

39. Ibid, no.226.

40. Ibid, no.267.

6

The Interregnum, 1650-1660

The Religious Revolution in Northenden and Etchells, 1640-1660

What the religious beliefs were of the majority of people in Northenden and Etchells in the seventeenth century is as difficult to ascertain as for most ordinary people in the country before the advent of universal literacy and opinion polls. Wills are a source from which it might be possible to reconstitute the religious views of a small part of the population (the well-to-do). But there are problems using wills. The words used at the beginning of the document (where the testator commends his soul to God and his body to a churchyard grave) might be only the usual form used by the parish/township clerk writing out the will. Therefore what seems like a community of Calvinists or Roman Catholics may be due to the fact that the clerk preferred that form of words or had a particular belief. Even so it is possible to pick out the unusual, such as Richard Goulden, gunsmith of Northenden, hoping to be one of the 'holy elect' in 1700 when such fervent religious protestation was long out of fashion. It can be safely assumed that Richard Goulden was a Presbyterian in 1700 and probably was in the 1640s and 1650s when he was a young man in his twenties and thirties. But it is less safe to assume that William Whitelegg of Gatley, also hoping to be one of the elect, was a Calvinist in 1642.[1]

Calvinism had been the prevalent belief amongst many Church of England clergy in the 1620s and continued to be common amongst clergymen into the 1660s, despite the fact that Charles I and Archbishop Laud favoured Armenianism to the point of harassing Calvinist clergy, such as William Bourne of Manchester, out of their livings and lectureships. Thomas Mallory, rector of Northenden, and Dr Nicholls were of the newer breed of clergy with leanings towards Armenianism and an acute awareness of the fact that there were more clergy with degrees than there were livings. Therefore, to some extent, clergymen needed to match their beliefs to those of their patrons, often the lord of the manor.

The majority of people in Northenden and Etchells probably paid lip-service to whoever was power and preaching from the pulpit of Northenden Church at the time (or Cheadle Church, which was nearer for those living in Gatley and Heathhouses) and kept their own personal beliefs private. But in the period 1648-1660 it must have been very difficult to tell who was in power. Was it Henry Dunster, Presbyterian rector of St Wilfrid's, who had the backing of the moderate Parliamentarians or Independents like Samuel Eaton and William Barrett, who had the backing of Colonel Robert Duckenfield and General Sir William Brereton? The dilemna reflected the political power struggle in Cheshire between the Deputy Lieutenants, the Booths and the radical Parliamentarians led by Brereton.

William Barrett held a tenement of Mrs Nicholls in Heathhouses, Etchells, was an agent for the Macclesfield Sequestrators and later, in 1650, a sub-commissioner for Cheshire with Henry Cockson. He provided a rival at-

traction to Northenden and Cheadle Churches at Ringway Chapel, which was only half a mile from the boundary of Shadow Moss and just over a mile's walking distance from most of the settlements and farms in southern Etchells and only two miles (a comfortable walking distance for the healthy) from Gatley and Northenden. Sir Peter Leycester, historian and Royalist, gave a description of Ringway Chapel in his *Historical Antiquities*.

> 'Here is a hamlet in Hale called Ringey, wherein is situated a chapel of ease, called Ringey chappel, within the parish of Bowdon; of which I have little to say, save that it was much frequented in the late war by schismatical ministers; and (was) as it were a receptacle for non-conformers in which dissolute times and very pragmatical illiterate person, as the humour served, stepped into the pulpit, without any lawful calling thereunto, or licence of authority.'[2]

Barrett and his congregation were revialled by local Presbyterians such as Adam Martindale of Rostherne, but Ringway survived beyond the Restoration and the Act of Uniformity whereas Martindale was expelled from his living. But even Barrett railed against the Quakers. In Manchester in the house of John Maddock, near the College buildings (now Chetham's Hospital) he tried to prove that the Quakers could not be 'saved'. When he could not Barrett had the constable run them out of Manchester.[3]

Barrett often had run-ins with his local Presbyterian opponents in his time at Ringway and prior to that as a preacher at Stockport under Samuel Eaton in 1652 and before. Henry Newcome, the Presbyterian minister at Gawsworth, who refused to attend a preaching exercise at Macclesfield purely because of Barrett's presence, called him a 'busy, pragmatical man'. The Plundered Ministers' Accounts Committee voted a yearly sum of £35 in 1646 towards the maintenance of the chapel and its preachers.[4]

The 'gathered congregation' at Ringway were part of a wider movement, although the number of Independent ministers in Cheshire were not large (Eaton and Timothy Taylor at Dunkenfield, Barrett at Ringway, George Moxon at Astbury and Jeremy Marsden at Neston). There were far larger numbers of Independent ministers within the area covered by the Manchester Presbyterian Classis.[5]

Quakers, like George Fox, Richard Hubberthorne and John Lawson, passed through or near Northenden and Etchells in the 1650s. Quaker meetings were certainly held in Wilmslow (a meeting house was built in Wilmslow after the Declaration of Toleration in 1673). Quakerism was a very attractive sect, especially to rural areas, so it possible that some meetings took place in Northenden or Etchells. After 1673 (or even before) they probably joined with the nearby Wilmslow Quakers.[6]

The Macclesfield Sequestrators were keen to see that the people of Northenden and Etchells were not without an approved minister with true Calvinist leanings even before the ejection of Thomas Mallory. Henry Root, who had been a preacher in Stockport in 1632, was brought in as part-time minister in 1643. Francis Shelmerdine and other ministers (Messrs. Chromich, Furnace, Marigold, Worsley, Hall and Bate) also preached occasionally at Northenden. Lecture days were also arranged where ministers would preach and debate before a congregation (the congregation were also supposed to join in the debates). At least three such lecture days took place in 1643, two before the siege of Wythenshawe Hall and one during. In 1645 Henry Dunster was appointed full-time minister. Henry Root was given a curacy at Sowerby, near Halifax on September 17th, 1646. Francis Shelmerdine was appointed Vicar of Mottram-in-Longendale in June 1651.[7]

Despite the ejection of her husband Mary Mallory and her six small children continued to live in Northenden, probably moving out of the Rectory into a small cottage which was part of the glebe lands some time in 1645 (another part of the glebe lands was in the hands of Captain Edmund Shelmerdine), and she was paid an allowance by the sequestrators.[8] Henry Dunster came to live at the Rectory in 1645 and he died there in 1662. He spent seventeen years in Northenden (more than Thomas Mallory would do), baptising his own children in St Wilfrid's along with those of his parishioners. According to his cousin, Henry Newcome, Dunster was a moderate man and very well-liked by his parishioners. He had some armour amongst his personal effects listed in the probate inventory, a back plate, breast plate and headpiece valued at £1.[9] Did Henry Dunster fight in the Civil Wars?

> [November 12th, 1661] 'Wee set out about 9. Got to Northerden [Northenden] before 11. Began soone after 11. I preached on Exod.XXX, 6, at ye baptisme of Felicia Dunstan [Dunster]. Wee had a deal of company: and saw ye free grace of God [tha]t we are not given up to ye some extreme vanitys & follys that others are. Alas how are some empty frothy ones of the gentry to be pittyed'.[10]

This was probably a comment on the dress and manners of some of the younger generation of Tattons. Mary, the eldest daughter, was then thirty-one and five years married, Anne was twenty-nine, but William was only twenty-five, Robert twenty-two and Thomas not yet twenty. Together with their cousins, the Leghs, they must have been a riotous bunch, as joyously fashionable as they could make themselves after the serious austerity of the 1650s.

Henry Dunster died on March 18th, 1662, just months before the Act of Uniformity would have forced him out of his living. Newcome wrote:

> 'I was, ... sent for by one from Northerden w[hi]ch acquainted mee w[i]th ye death of my cozen Dunster w[i]th desire to mee to preach his funerall on Thursda: A sad breach it is.'

And on Thursday, March 20th.

> 'Come to Northerden before 1. I preached at ye funeral of Mr. Dunster on 1 Ks xx, 1, w[he]re was much lamentation made. Poore family and poore people!'[11]

Although the parish of Northenden was not part of the Manchester Presbyterian Classis, Henry Dunster did occasionally attend the Classis meetings. On August 17th, 1659 he preached on 2 Kings IX 'What peace? So long as the whoredoms of thy mother Jezebel and her witchcrafts are so many?'. Strong stuff and probably needed in the confused times of the Rump, after the death of Oliver Cromwell and before the Restoration of Charles II. Dunster also preached elsewhere. On January 18th, 1661, he preached at Stockport in the place of his cousin, Henry Newcome, who was ill.[12] When Newcome was again preaching at Stockport on February 21st, 1662, Dunster, returning from London (just a month before his death), joined him, John Angier and Samuel Eaton.[13] Dunster had probably been taking part in the delicate negotiations between the Presbyterian Assembly of Divines, Charles II and the ejected Anglican clergymen.

Henry Cockson, Solicitor for Sequestrations in Cheshire, as an elder of Manchester Parish Church and personal friend of many Presbyterian ministers, also preached occasionally at Classis meetings. He preached at a Classis meeting at Knutsford on November 25th, 1656. He was one of those who were instrumental in getting Henry Newcome elected to the parish of Manchester in December 1656 following the death of Richard Hollinworth.[14]

Dr Thomas Mallory resumed his occupancy of Northenden Rectory not long after the death of Henry Dunster (Newcome and Cockson helped his widow sell off her husband's £20 worth of books, possibly after she had moved out of the rectory). Unlike many other ejected Anglican clergy, Mallory returned without benefit of the Act of Uniformity. Perhaps because of this he retained good relations with Presbyterian ministers like Henry Newcome who even called him 'my friend' when Mallory had a word with the Bishop of Chester about offering Newcome a parish if he accepted the Act of Uniformity. However, Newcome did not think much of Mallory's preaching style.

> [November 9th, 1662] 'Dr. Mallory preached on 1 Cor.IX 26, a learned unprofitable sermon to ye generality of ye people. Though it occasioned no griefe as was feared. If ye shepheard fed not as was desired, yet ye watchman smote not as was feared.'[15]

What lasting effects did twenty years of religious ferment leave on the people of Northenden and Etchells? The greatest effect here, as elsewhere, was that the people no longer were forced through sheer lack of choice to listen to the preaching of the rector in Northenden Church (or Cheadle Church either, for those in the township of Stockport Etchells). Although made almost illegal by the Clarendon Code, Ringway Chapel and the Wilmslow Quakers continued on after the Restoration. Neither the Independents nor the Quakers had been fully part of the Presbyterian State Church. So the failure to come to an agreement with the returning Anglican clergy was not as catatrophic to them as it was to the Presbyterian clergy who suddenly found themselves outside the Church of England. Therefore they just carried on as they had always done. John Brereton, Presbyterian minister of Wilmslow and kinsman of Sir William Brereton, took over Ringway Chapel after his ejection.[16] So Ringway became a Presbyterian chapel, both its congregation and its minister, breaking laws in the Clarendon Code left, right and centre and seemingly triumphing against all persecutors into the early eighteenth century. John Brereton even had religious meetings at his own house at Castle Mill, near Ashley. For other ejected Presbyterian ministers like Francis Shelmerdine of Chamber Hall life after the Act of Uniformity was difficult. Shelmerdine made the very astute move of setting himself up as a weaver/clothier to keep his family and trained his two younger sons, Matthew and James as weaver/clothiers too.[17] Shelmerdine, like John Brereton, also held religious meetings in Chamber Hall, and perhaps even took services at Ringway Chapel, as other ministers seem to have done. After the Declaration of Indulgence in 1673 Shelmerdine openly established Chamber Hall as a meeting house for Presbyterian services by hanging a chapel bell out of the side of one of the walls at the back of the hall.[18]

The shock of being thrust outside the Church of England and the persecution which followed was almost too much for the Presbyterians. The 1673 Declaration of Indulgence did not halt the decline of Presbyterianism. Even Ringway Chapel was forcibly closed in the end in 1721 and another building erected and licensed for worship in Hale. This was further away from its Northenden and Etchells devotees, but by then Francis Shelmerdine had established his meeting place. Although he died the year after the Declaration of Indulgence, arrangements seem to have been made to continue Chamber Hall as a meeting place at least until it was sold by the widow of Francis's grandson, Matthew.[19] Those Presbyterian meeting houses, like the one at Hale, which survived into the mid-eighteenth century were converted to Unitarian beliefs and became 'chapels'.

The Tattons, 1650-1660 and after the Restoration

Life in the 1650s gradually eased slightly for the Tattons, as it did for their tenants and friends. Henry Cockson continued in the post of Solicitor for Sequestrations in Cheshire and continued to fight for the Tattons and their relatives through his contacts until 1659. The radical, personal influence of Sir William Brereton was largely removed from Cheshire life after Parliament awarded him Archbishop Laud's palace at Croydon for his military services and as he became more and more involved in central government. Cheshire returned to the rule of the more moderate Deputy Lieutenants, including the Booths and the Mainwarings. But Cromwell, despite former friendship, turned both Brereton and Lord President Bradshawe (Brereton's nominee) out of office when he became Lord Protector in 1653.[20]

In 1652 Cheshire lost one of its oldest and most influential local politicians, Sir George Booth of Dunham, at the grand old age of eighty-six. Born in 1566 when Elizabeth was a young queen, he was one of the last survivors of that age. 'Free, grave, godly Booth, the flower of Cheshire', the pamphleteers called him. He was succeeded at Dunham Hall by his grandson, George Booth, an impetuous and reckless man of twenty-nine, in the

mould of his handsome, arrogant uncle, Colonel John Booth.[21]

There were two more brief Civil Wars in 1648 (when the battle of Preston took place and Colonel John Booth turned coat and tried to take Chester for the King) and in 1651 (when Charles Stuart tried to invade England with an army of Scots and which ended in the battle of Worcester). Robert Tatton, now forty-five and struggling with debts and fines, took no part in either the 1648 or the 1651 Civil War. Even so he was, was mentioned in the last chapter, fined in 1651 both as an ex-Royalist and to pay for the fight against Charles Stuart and his forces.

From 1653 onwards Cheshire, along with Staffordshire and Lancashire, came under the rule of one of the most zealous of the Major Generals. Charles Worsley was the son of a Manchester clothier, who brought Platt Hall in Rusholme, just south of Manchester, in the early seventeenth century. Worsley saw Royalist plots in every bush and ruthlessly introduced the Decimation Tax on all former delinquents in his area. There is no record of how much Robert was fined but it is unlikely that he escaped paying a sizeable amount.

Worsley's rule lasted three years, until his death from overwork in 1656. His successor, Tobias Bridge, had two great advantages as far as the local gentry were concerned. He was a moderate and he was a stranger, with no intimate knowledge of their relationships and intrigues as Worsley had had.

Although Worsley's rule was comparatively short, historians have claimed that he made possible the return of the old social order. Former Royalists and Presbyterians (some of the latter were under suspicion and imprisoned at the time of the Third Civil War) came together to oppose him.[22] The outcome was the amalgamation of both parties in the abortive rising of Sir George Booth in August 1659. Robert Tatton himself did not take part in the rising but he did approve his eldest son William, now twenty-three years old, becoming one of Sir George Booth's officers. He probably also approved the action of William Whitelegg of Northenden, the township constable for 1659, in hiring four soldiers to go with Sir George Booth's troops under the command of Colonel Legh of Adlington Hall (the son of Sir Thomas Legh). Robert Tatton the younger was probably an ensign under Colonel Legh too. He captured by Colonel Lambert's troops after the battle of Winnington Bridge (just north of Northwich), on August 19th, 1659. There is no mention of what happened to the four soldiers at Winnington Bridge.[23]

The pamphleteers had a field-day after the fiasco of Winnington Bridge and its aftermath when Sir George Booth escaped disguised as a woman.

"From Sir George Booth and his Cheshire lies,
From being taken in disguise,
From those that send us that devil, Excise,
Good Lord deliver us!"[24]

Changes were taking place in the Tatton family. The five surviving children grew up under the shadow of the Civil War and the Interregnum. Mary, the eldest daughter, married Charles Wheeler, gentleman. According to Earwaker, Wheeler died in 1658, but he was alive enough in 1665 to witness the sale of Vawdrey lands in Northenden by Samuel Vawdrey (either the son of Henry Vawdrey of Hazelhurst or the son of Robert Vawdrey of Riddings, Timperley) to William Tatton (probably on the occasion of his marriage to the heiress, Anne Eyre of Bradway in Derbyshire).[25] Anne, the second daughter, did not marry until 1665 when she was thirty-three.[26] Most of the children did not marry until after the Restoration, except Mary, perhaps because the Tattons' fortunes were still on the wane or because the times were still so unsettled.

A number of deaths took place amongst the close relatives of the Tattons. Anne's eldest brother Richard died on September 14th, 1649, leaving his estates divided between his second and youngest brothers, Thomas and Peter. The latter died in 1659, mercifully before the Restoration, otherwise he might have suffered greatly for his part in the Interregnum. When Thomas died in 1660 the Ashley lands were divided between the three surviving sisters, Anne, Frances and Katherine. Anne's and Frances's share was given as a marriage portion to Anne, the second daughter in 1665.

1649 was also the year in which Robert' uncle, James Massey of Sale, died. In 1656 Anne's brother-in-law Alexander Barlowe died. The following year Dr Nicholls died at the age of sixty-six.

"William Nicholls, Dr. of Divinity exchanged this lyfe for a better upon Wed. morning the 16th Dec. and was buryed in the middle of the South Chapel at Northenden on Sat. 19th of the same month in the yeare 1657'.[27]

William Tatton, now twenty, moved into Peele Hall, soon after the death of Dr Nicholls, to both help his grandmother farm the Peele demesne lands and to give the young man experience of running an estate under the watchful eye of his father. He continued running the dower lands after his grandmother's death in January 1666 (at the great age of eighty). Unfortunately he had only four years after the death of his father before his own demise in 1673. He left a young widow, a son of five and a daughter only just turned four (a second son, William, had died aged six months old a few months before his father). From then on until the end of the century the two manors were ruled by a succession of minors and their guardians.[28]

Robert, the second son, married Anne the daughter of Peter Davenport of Bramhall (son of William Davenport), and lived at Stockport, Cheetham Hill and Ardwick in Manchester (land inherited from his father). He died and was buried at Stockport in 1686 at the age of fifty-seven, just a few days before his brother-in-law, Robert Radcliffe. His eldest son, William, eventually inherited the two manors. Thomas, the third son, who married Mary, the daughter of Edward Pegg of Beauchief, Derbyshire, held a small tenement in Northenden and lived at Peele Hall until his death in 1692 at the age of fifty.

Despite the debts and the deaths, Robert Tatton's family did make some gains from the Civil War and the Interregnum which were to be the saving of the family and their estates from 1673 to the end of the century. The Court of Wards and Livery, that pernicious tax on orphans and widows with estates from which Robert Tatton, Colonel Duckenfield and Sir William Brereton had all suffered, was abolished early in the life of the Long Parliament. Since there were two more minors inheriting the estates between 1673 and 1690 the Tattons were saved a great deal of money and trouble. It also meant that William Tatton's widow could remarry four years after the death of her husband, rather than wait until her son was twenty-one to do so, as Mrs Katherine Nicholls had been forced to do.

The Interregnum introduced a law of Strict Settlement, which meant that no heir could sell off his patrimony. Whether that helped the Tattons or not is not certain since the heirs, where they attained their majority, were intent on expanding their lands not selling them off. But it did mean that they were accountable to a number of trustees, which at one time included a creditor, John Crewe of Crewe.[29]

What of those who thought they would gain a great deal through the Civil War and the Interregnum, the Parliamentarians of Northenden and Etchells? Francis Shelmerdine's ejection from his living has already been mentioned. Henry Cockson, who as a Presbyterian, probably approved, even if he felt himself too aged to take part, of Sir George Booth's abortive rising. He continued as Steward of the Court Leet of Northenden and Etchells until his death in 1666. He gained great local and some national influence through his position as Solicitor for Sequestrations during the Civil War Period. On the Restoration he lost his national influence but his local influence remained as great as ever it was, at least amongst Presbyterians like Henry Newcome and his relatives.

However, there were others who thought they lost a great deal more than they gained, the poorer men who had believed they would have 'the Norman yoke' removed from them when Charles I's head was severed from his body. Disillusionment came soon after and some were very bitter at the Restoration. Edmund Shelmerdine, the former captain in Colonel Duckenfield's and later Colonel Bradshawe's regiments, was arrested for speaking seditious and treasonable words in a Northenden alehouse, perhaps The Boat.

'there never was such great taxes laid upon the country as now there were, and that there would never be peace and quietness till they did as they did in Germany and that is to rise and cut the throats of the gentry in England, wherein he [Edmund Shelmerdine] said he will be as ready as any man...they hate the name of a gentleman to this day.'[30]

Did Shelmerdine mean just Royalist gentry like the Tattons or did he include Parliamentarian gentry, like Sir George Booth, who turned Royalist after Oliver Cromwell's death in 1658, tried, albeit very unsuccessfully, to bring about the Restoration in 1659 and was given the title Baron of Delamere for his pains? But poor yeomen and husbandmen like Edmund Shelmerdine did not have the wealth or the local influence to be able to ride out the adverse times. He and four others were found guilty of sedition before the General Sessions in Chester in October 1662 (there were many others also found guilty of sedition in Cheshire both before and after Shelmerdine). He was put in the stocks at Chester for an hour, stripped half-naked, beaten out of town before being imprisoned in the castle until his fine was paid. He died in 1674, the same year as his kinsman, Francis Shelmerdine of Chamber Hall.[31]

Notes

1. The Wills of Richard Goulden (1700) and William Whitelegg (1642), CCRO.
2. From Sir Peter Leycester's *Historical Antiquities*, published originally in 1674, quoted in *A History of Hale, Cheshire* edited by R.N. Dore, John Sherratt and Sons.
3. 'Historical Notes on the Society of Friends of Quakers in Manchester in the 17th Century', *LCAS*, Vol. 31, 1913, p.49-50.
4. Alfred Tarbolton, *Ringway Chapel before the Disruption, 1515-1721*, p.32.
5. *The Civil Wars in Cheshire*, p.83.
6. *Cheshire 1660-1780*, p.35-37.
7. Accounts of Expenditure for Northenden Parish from Macclesfield Sequestration Committee, BL Harleian MSS 2180, f.134 and f.209, quoted in Earwaker; *Calamy Revised*.
8. Accounts of Expenditure for Northenden Parish from Macclesfield Sequestration Committee, BL Harleian MSS2180, and BL Harleian MSS 2130, quoted in Earwaker, vol.1, p.293.
9. Probate inventory of Henry Dunster of Northenden, clerk, CCRO.
10. *The Diary of Henry Newcome*, Chet. Soc., Vol.18, p.19.
11. Ibid, pp.68-69.
12. *Autobiography of Henry Newcome*, parts 1 and 2, Chet. Soc., O.S., vols 26 and 27, pp.112 and 135.
13. *The Diary of Henry Newcome*, p.59.
14. *Autobiography*, pp.63, 337, 352.
15. *Autobiography*, p.152; *The Diary of Henry Newcome*, p.138.
16. *A History of Hale*, p.39-40.
17. The probate inventory and will of Francis Shelmerdine of Chamber Hall, clerk, 1674, CCRO. Matthew Shelmerdine became a clothier with a shop in Stockport.
18. It can still be seen at Chamber Hall.
19. *Wythenshawe: to 1926*, p.189; the will of Matthew Shelmerdine dated 1733, CCRO. It was first sold to the Reverend Twyford of Didsbury, then in 1756 to William Tatton of Wythenshawe.
20. *Cheshire 1630-1660*, pp.183-4.
21. *Cheshire in the Civil Wars*, p.92.
22. *Cheshire 1630-1660*, pp.276-287.
23. *Wythenshawe: to 1926*, pp.116-17, William Whitelegg (he is called 'Whiteley' in the Quarter Sessions Records – a mis-transcription) seems to have been left with the charge of the four soldiers. In October 1660, after Whitelegg asked the Quarter Sessions Court for permission to get the men to desert or raise the money in a ley from Northenden inhabitants, the constables collected the money to pay the soldiers.
24. See *Cheshire in the Civil Wars*, pp.90-95 for a full account of this abortive, and at times, farcial Royalist/Presbyterian rising.
25. Earwaker, Tatton Family Tree. It is very possible that the Charles Wheeler who died in 1658 was father to the Charles Wheeler who was alive in 1665 and that Mary married the son and not the father. Whatever the truth she was a widow by 1677.
26. Her uncle Thomas Brereton had made her heiress to a third of the Ashley estates on his death in 1663(?) and so, despite her 31 years, she was a very eligible catch for Sir Amos Meredith of Ashley. She bore him children and outlived him to remarry Sir Samuel Daniell of Tabley and die an old lady of 76 in 1708.
27. Northenden Parish Register, quoted in *Wythenshawe: to 1926*, p.173.
28. William's widow, Anne, went on to remarry Robert Radcliffe, second son to the ardent Royalist, Sir Alexander Radcliffe of Ordsall Hall in Salford (see Chapter 2). By him she had four more children, two sons and two daughters. Robert Radcliffe was killed in a duel on Bowdon Downs in February, 1686. William's heir, Robert, who was engaged to Frances Legh of Lyme Hall, died in the year he reached twenty-one and took over the running of the two manors from his mother. The estate then passed to William Tatton, the eldest son and heir of Robert, the second son. He lived on until 1732 and began some of the great changes in the eighteenth century which were to turn the two manors from a community of copyholders to one of freeholders paying miminal rent and able to mortgage and properly sell their tenements and the Tatton estates as a whole from land that just about kept the family in meat and other household provision to a profit-making concern, increasing in size and influence. His son, also William, married Hester, sister and heiress to Samuel Egerton of Tatton and gained those estates on the death of the latter, bought the manor of Baguley, land in Werneth Low on the border of Derbyshire and Golborne Hall in Lancashire as well as increasing the number of leaseholders in Northenden and Etchells, paying economic rent from one to over thirty. The father had shown the way by selling off the tenements to the copyholders and renting Peele Hall and the demesne land to any who could farm it and pay the rent.
29. John Crewe owned a large proportion of the manor of Hale, which bordered the manor of Etchells, near the Shadow Moss. Therefore he had practical agricultural reasons as well as purely economic ones for being a Tatton trustee.
30. From Cheshire Quarter Sessions Records, quoted in *Cheshire, 1660-1780*, p.3.
31. Wills proved at Chester 1660-1680, LCRS, vol. 15.

Bibliography

PRIMARY SOURCES

MANUSCRIPT SOURCES

Tatton Family Papers, John Rylands Library, Manchester

1648 Rental Survey (document no. 195)
1656/7 Rental Survey (document no. 347)
Bond between Mrs Katherine Nicholls and Edmund Joydrell of Yeardsley dated 1626 (document no. 213)
Discharge of a debt for £100, dated 1636 (document no. 378)
Documents to do with the Court of Wards and Liveries 1635-40 (documents no. 258, 378 and 380).
Northenden Court Leet/Court Baron Records 1667-1700 (document no.339).
1670 Rental Survey (document no. 342).
Grant of Northen Parks to Richard Brereton in part payment of a debt (document no. 1284).
Bond from Thomas Brereton of the Inner Temple, London for lending £70 to Robert Tatton dated may 3rd, 1636 (documents no. 398-400).
The Deposition of James Brownhill, dated 1646.
Inventory of the contents of Wythenshawe Hall dated 1644 (also printed in *Wythenshawe: to 1926*).
'The Boke of Ye Trayned bandes of Cheshire' (document no. 282).
A copy of a deposition from the Tatton composition papers in the PRC.
1699 Rental Survey (document no. 337).
Rental of Dr. Nicholls, dated 1643/44.
Bond and counterbond between Robert Tatton, Dr Nicholls and Lord Cholmondley (document no.222).

Printed safe-conduct passes dated June 1646 and December 1646 (document nos. 285 and 286).
Hand-written safe-conduct passes July 1646 and March 1646/7.
19th century copy of a letter written by Anne Tatton in the PRO (document no.287).
Letter from Sir Thomas Fairfax for the Macclesfield Sequestration Committee dated October 1647.
Draft of deed for lease of the demesne lands.
Letters between Robert Tatton, his brother-in-law, Peter Brereton, Peter's cousin, Basil Hearne and Henry Cockson (documents nos. 227, 266, 267, 269).
Rough draft and fair copy of mortgage deed made before Oliver St John, Chief Justice of the Court of Common Bench dated December, 1656 (document no. 1106).
Survey of Wythenshawe Demesne, c.1700 (document no.338a).

Other manuscript sources

Public Records Office State Papers (PRO SP) Vol 149.
Cheshire County Record Office (CCRO) Cowper MSS, Vol 2, f1.
Will and inventory of Richard Goulden of Northern Moor, gunsmith, dated 1700, CCRO
Central Library Archives, Manchester, Etchells Court Leet/Court Baron Records 1660-1730 (document no. M10/20/2b).
The unpublished transcript of the first volume of Northenden Parish Register.

PRINTED PRIMARY SOURCES

Distraint for Knighthood, The Record Society of Lancashire and Cheshire (LCRS) Vol 12.
LCRS, Vol 95.
Cheshire Inquisition Post-Mortems, 1630-1660, *LCRS*, Vol 91.
Cheshire Quarter Sessions, LCRS, Vol 94.
The Letter Books of Sir William Brereton, edited by R.N. Dore, published by LCRS, Vol 123 (1984).
Civil War Tracts of Lancashire, G. Ormerod, Chetham Society, Vol 2.
1641 map of Northenden, modern facsimile by Frank and Teretta Mitchell.
Letters of Humphrey Chetham and to Humphrey Chetham, Manchester clothier, printed in *Life of Humphrey Chetham*, Chetham Society, New Series, Vols 49 and 50.
Manchester Court Leet Records, Vol IV.
Didsbury Protestation Return, dated February, 1642 – Warden Heyricke's Protestation – printed in *A New History of Didsbury* by Francis Woodall.
St James', Didsbury, Parish Register, published by the Parish Register Society of Lancashire and Cheshire, Vol 1, Part 1, (1900).
Wythenshawe garrison list, Assessment for delinquency fine, BL Harleian MS 2130 Accounts for the parsonage lands of St Wilfrid's, Northenden and Expenditure for Northenden Parish from the Macclesfield Sequestration Committee, printed in *East Cheshire*, JP Earwaker, Vol 1,

published in 1879.
Memorials of the Civil Wars in Cheshire, J. Hall, LCRS, Vol 19.
Warrant of Lord Byron, St. Oswald's Register, Chester, parish register of St Mary-on-the-Hill, BL Harleian MS 2155, three letters of Robert Tatton and Charles Walley to Sir William Brereton, all printed in *Siege of Chester*, J Morris, Journal of the Chester and North Wales Archaeological Society (JCNWAS), 1923.
Two letters between Lord Byron and Sir William Brereton, Randle Holmes's account of the damage done to Chester printed in Ormerod's *History of Cheshire*, Vol 1.
Cheshire Civil War Tracts, Chetham Society, New Series, Vol 65.
The Diary of the Reverend Henry Newcome, Chetham Society, Vol 7, 1849.
Life of Adam Martindale, Chetham Society, Old Series, Vol 4.
Autobiography of Henry Newcome, Chetham Society, Old Series, Vols 26 and 27.
Calendar of Proceedings of the Committee for Compounding
Calendar of Proceedings of the Committee for the Advancement of Money.

SECONDARY SOURCES

Local books

W.H.Shercliff, editor — *Wythenshawe: to 1926*, E.J. Morten, Didsbury, Manchester, 1974.

J.S.Morrill, — *Cheshire 1630-1660: County Government and Society during the 'English Revolution'*, Oxford University Press, Monograph Series.
The Revolt of the Provinces.

Dr George Ormerod — *History of Cheshire*, Vols I and III.

E. Broxap — *The Great Civil War in Lancashire*, Manchester University Press, 1910.

R.N. Dore — *The Great Civil War in the Manchester Area.*
The Civil Wars in Cheshire, Vol 8, History of Cheshire Series, Cheshire Community Council, 1966.

R.N. Dore and J.S. Morrill — *The Allegiance of the Cheshire Gentry*, Transactions of the Lancashire and Cheshire Antiquarian Society (TLCAS), Vol 77.

J.Howard Hodson — *Cheshire, 1660-1780: Restoration of Industrial Revolution*, Vol 9, History of Cheshire Series, Cheshire Community Council, 1978.

Joyce Littler, — 'A Commentary on the 1701 Estate Survey and the Rentals of 1704 and 1709 of Dunham Massey' (1992), Altrincham Library.

Robert Muschamp — 'Historical Notes on the Society of Friends of Quakers in Manchester in the 17th century', *TLCAS*, Vol 31, 1913.

Alfred Tarbolton — *Ringway Chapel before the Disruption, 1515-1721.*

National books

Christopher Hill — *Century of Revolution*, Nelson, second edition, 1980.

A.C.Matthews, editor — *Walker Revised: Being a Revision of John Walker's Sufferings of the Clergy During the Grand Rebellion 1642-1660*, Oxford University Press, 1948.
Calamy Revised, 1642-1662, Oxford University Press.

Colonel H.C.B Rogers — *Weapons of the British Soldier*, Seeley, Service and Co. Ltd, 1960.

Harold L. Peterson — *The Book of the Gun*, Hamlyn, 1963.

B. Scholfield, editor — *The Knyett Letters*, Norfolk Record Society, Vol 20.

Peter Clark — *The English Alehouse: A Social History 1200 to 1830.*